T0339509

Integrating Technology in English Language Arts Teacher Education

Integrating Technology in English Language Arts Teacher Education investigates the technology practices teacher candidates in the US are being introduced to, how they are using these practices in classrooms, and how technology can be effectively integrated into English teacher education programs.

By drawing upon findings from extensive longitudinal studies into teacher education programs in the US, this timely volume addresses critical themes relating to the integration of technology in education, including:

- Teaching with technology
- Technology for collaboration
- Technology for individualized learning and assessment

By analyzing the experiences of teacher educators and candidates, and offering detailed analysis of the content, practices, and skills being taught to pre-service English teachers, Pasternak examines the entities that drive or inhibit the adoption of technology into the secondary English language arts (ELA) curriculum.

This volume will resonate with an international audience of post-graduate scholars and researchers interested in the fields of teacher education, English language arts, and the relationship between technology and classroom practice.

Donna L. Pasternak is Professor of English Education in the Department of Teaching and Learning in the School of Education at the University of Wisconsin-Milwaukee, USA. She is the site director for the University of Wisconsin-Milwaukee Writing Project, an affiliate of the National Writing Project.

Routledge Research in Teacher Education

The Routledge Research in Teacher Education series presents the latest research on Teacher Education and also provides a forum to discuss the latest practices and challenges in the field.

Research on Becoming an English Teacher
Through Lacan's Looking Glass
Tony Brown, Mike Dore and Christopher Hanley

Intercultural Competence in the Work of Teachers
Confronting Ideologies and Practices
Edited by Fred Dervin, Robyn Moloney and Ashley Simpson

Teacher Representations in Dramatic Text and Performance
Portraying the Teacher on Stage
Edited by Melanie Shoffner and Richard St. Peter

School-Based Deliberative Partnership as a Platform for Teacher Professionalization and Curriculum Innovation
Geraldine Mooney Simmie and Manfred Lang

Technology-Enabled Mathematics Education
Optimising Student Engagement
Catherine Attard and Kathryn Holmes

Integrating Technology in English Language Arts Teacher Education
Donna L. Pasternak

For more information about this series, please visit: www.routledge.com/
Routledge-Research-in-Teacher-Education/book-series/RRTE

Integrating Technology in English Language Arts Teacher Education

Donna L. Pasternak

Routledge
Taylor & Francis Group

NEW YORK AND LONDON

First published 2020
by Routledge
605 Third Avenue, New York, NY 10017

and by Routledge
2 Park Square, Milton Park, Abingdon, Oxon, OX14 4RN

First issued in paperback 2021

Routledge is an imprint of the Taylor & Francis Group, an informa business

Library of Congress Cataloging-in-Publication Data
A catalog record for this book has been requested

ISBN 13: 978-1-03-223949-1 (pbk)
ISBN 13: 978-1-138-35951-2 (hbk)

Typeset in Times New Roman
by Apex CoVantage, LLC

For Helen,

your impossible, my possible

Contents

Tables

Acknowledgments

After years of attending the Methods Commission meetings at the annual conference of the National Council of Teachers of English's (NCTE) affiliate English Language Arts Teacher Educators' (ELATE, formerly CEE) group, I met Laura Renzi and reestablished my friendship with Samantha Caughlan as they took over the commission's leadership. Through my participation in that commission, I met Leslie S. Rush and solidified my friendship and mentorship of another member, Heidi L. Hallman.

In leading the Methods Commission, Laura and Sam had some big idea that we needed to replicate, revise, expand, and update Peter Smagorinsky and Melissa Whiting's study of English teacher education in the United States, published in 1995 as *How English Teachers Get Taught: Methods of Teaching the Methods Class*. Their study was considered the standard of understanding English teacher education up until 2018—the date when Sam and Laura's big idea came to fruition with the publication of our own study of that content, *Secondary English Teacher Education in the United States*.

Little did I know then that Sam, Heidi, Laura, Leslie, and I would collaborate, support each other, and play together for almost a decade, moving us beyond and across academia to find niches in field experience, standards, literacy, second language, and technology English language arts scholarship. Without each of you, this new book, *Integrating Technology in English Language Arts Teacher Education*, would not have been possible. I thank you all for your contribution to my intellectual growth and well-being. I especially thank Samantha Caughlan for reading *every* word of this book. Your critical eye is the sharpest. Your breadth of knowledge the widest. Thank you for sharing that with me.

In taking this scholarly journey together, the five of us met some pretty extraordinary people and had some remarkable opportunities come our way that supported the writing of this book. Thus, I acknowledge the following contributions:

The NCTE ELATE leadership and members who helped shape the original study and develop the contact list of participants, which led to the data discussed in this book. I especially acknowledge the study participants who muscled through the technology content, submitted their syllabi for analysis, and spoke candidly about the rewards and challenges of integrating technology across an English teacher education program. I thank Dr. Bruce E. Spitzer, Professor of Education and Chairperson, Department of Education, North Central College, who voluntarily provided feedback on his syllabus, course, and program design. I acknowledge the work recently done with Dr. Heidi L. Hallman and Dr. Kristen Pastore-Capuana, the new chairs of the ELATE Methods Commission, and Dr. Julie Bell, for critical feedback and conversations about technology integration and English teacher education.

Support was provided by the University of Wisconsin-Milwaukee (UWM) Graduate School and School of Education; UWM's Research Growth Initiative Grant; UWM's Office of Undergraduate Research; Dr. Hope Longwell-Grice, Associate Dean of UWM's School of Education; and then-graduate student researchers Dr. Hannah Meineke and Dr. Danielle Hartke DeVasto; graduate student researchers Molly Ubbesen and Angie Henegar; and undergraduate student researcher Erica Shavon Woods.

I am particularly indebted to Dr. Candance Doerr-Stevens for convincing me there is a need to follow-up on earlier technology studies of the University of Wisconsin-Milwaukee English teacher education program. We are now looking at competence and confidence of teacher candidates in relation to programmatic commitments.

Lastly, I thank the University of Wisconsin-Milwaukee English teacher education students. Your willingness to learn and become activist educators is beyond compare. It is an honor to say I am your teacher.

Thank you to Peter Smagorinsky and Melissa Whiting for your foundational study (1995), which allowed me to envision a picture of technology integration across a program.

The editors and anonymous reviewers of my articles and books who helped me sharpen my arguments at Routledge, Taylor & Francis Group; Rowman and Littlefield; Bloomsbury Academic; and *Contemporary Issues in Technology and Teacher Education*.

I would be remiss in not acknowledging my mother, Helen Pasternak, and my siblings, Robyn Guy, Steven Pasternak, and Scott Pasternak and their families. Thank you does not seem enough when you consider that over the years you read countless pages; listened to shards of developing arguments, oftentimes by walking me miles through the woods; and even shopped for groceries and washed my laundry when the need arose. I am one lucky person to come from such a strong, loving family.

And then there's Stanley B. Shulfer. Your love sustains me as you sustain our lives. Together we are all possibilities.

1   Integrating Technology Into the English Language Arts

Teachers in today's English language arts classrooms must be proficient in understanding and teaching how multimodal literacies and technology integration are integral aspects of the discipline (CEE Executive Committee, 2008; Hamilton, Hydon, Hibbert, & Stooke, 2015), aspects that continue to change literacy practices with every adaptation of hardware and software, affecting not only the content of the English language arts classroom but its instruction as well. These changes to the field are not unique to the teaching of English in the United States. Goodwyn (2012) predicts that "The Future" in English teaching in England is "predicated on a model of English operating in a multimodal, digital environment in which students are fully engaged in a creative relationship with reading and writing all kinds of texts" (p. 299). If English teachers remain the educators responsible for teaching literacy practices (Wilson, 2011), and Goodwyn's predictions are right, changing literacy practices will continue to affect the content of English as a core subject in education. This book identifies the main tensions across the field of English teacher education that develop when teacher educators attempt to integrate technology into the teaching of English. It explores which practices are taught in the methods (teaching practices) course, the course designated as the location teacher candidates learn to teach English.

The English language arts methods, teaching practices class is defined as the course in teacher education that focuses on the representation and teaching of English language arts content and involves the inquiry into the beliefs or opinions of its participants regarding concepts of the English language arts at the secondary and middle school levels, the planning of lessons or courses of study, and classroom management related to the subject-area methods (Pasternak, Caughlan, Hallman, Renzi, & Rush, 2018). Subject-specific methods courses are considered the primary location where middle and secondary teachers develop subject-matter-specific pedagogical content knowledge (Ball, Thames, & Phelps, 2008; Shulman, 1987).

With a focus on methods course content, this book draws on data (questionnaire, course syllabi, focus groups, and case studies) from the first extensive research-based study since 1995 of how secondary English teachers have been educated at institutions of higher education in the US. Chapters address the analysis of the content, practices, and skills being taught to teacher candidates in their methods courses as they negotiate the teaching and learning of technology in the English language arts methods course, offering English teachers, English language arts educators, and teacher educators in other disciplines a template from which to view technology integration and its capacity to change literacy practices. The book identifies and examines practices taught to teacher candidates by English teacher educators and the struggles they encounter to integrate technology effectively into their literacy instruction, exploring the barriers and supports that may prevent or foster change, and examining the entities that drive or inhibit technology's adoption.

The study and teaching of the English language arts has changed from a field that defines itself through the teaching of literature, composition, and oratory (Dixon, 1967) to one that now instructs in the skills needed to study that content: reading, writing, listening, speaking, and critical thinking (Moje, 2008). How will the teaching of technology and its interrelationship within the English language arts continue to change the field? This book aims to explore the practices and thinking behind those relationships to provide insight into what it means to integrate technology into the English language arts.

English Language Arts in the United States

Teaching English in countries where the English language is the dominant mode of communication often means instruction in language acquisition, awareness, and proficiency. However, in the United States, this content is taught under the term second language acquisition (Pasternak et al., 2018). When *English* or *language arts* or *English studies* have been taught in the United States, the subject generally means instruction in the English language through the study of a diverse range of literary texts, compositional modes, linguistics, culture, humanities, and oratory in alignment with the skills needed to master those topics: reading, writing, listening, critical thinking, and speaking (Hook, 1962; Randel, 1958; Smagorinsky, 2015). Correspondingly, instruction in English has had different purposes over the years, including "[S]haping values, to creating a democratic citizenry, to developing cognitive abilities, to preparing students for college and careers, and to enable students to strive toward other societal goals" (Pasternak et al., 2018, p. 7).

In recent years, the discipline has come to an awareness that technology is changing and will continue to change how people communicate (George, Pope, & Reid, 2015; Hawthorne et al., 2012), thus placing pressure on English teacher educators to integrate this content into their methods (teaching practices) classes.

Integrating Technology Into the English Language Arts: A Definition

Research shows (Pasternak et al., 2018) that technology integration should underscore the learning of conceptual knowledge, procedural knowledge, and attitudinal and/or value-based knowledge specific to the content of a discipline (Guzman & Nussbaum, 2009). When integrated across a teacher education program, technology should become a tool for learning (Gorder, 2008; Harris, Mishra, & Koehler, 2009) that supports instructional practices (Ertmer, 2005) and is integral to the learning process (Pierson, 2001). Thus, in an English teacher education program, technology not only supports the learning of the traditional English language arts content, but also becomes new content when the software and/or hardware must be learned to engage the traditional content—acting interdependently to create new knowledge and new tasks (Hsieh, 2018; Mirra, 2018; Rowsell, Morrell, & Alvermann, 2017).

Incorporating technology content into the English language arts teacher education program has become an uneven endeavor considering that many individuals entering the field do so to teach its more traditional content of literature, language, oratory, and composition (Pasternak, 2007; Thieman, 2008). Effectively integrating technology and valuing it as a practice has created tensions within the English teacher education community (Pasternak et al., 2016): finding expertise in the teaching of the English language arts in addition to expertise in understanding technology platforms and applications; accommodating the unequal and, sometimes, suspect funding of technology across and between school districts and universities; locating the common ground between valuing technology in the classroom and coming to terms with its ability to both distract or engage learners; establishing consistent technology policies in schools; and using standards to drive effective technology integration and usage in education.

Moreover, when integrating technology into the English language arts, it should be considered that technologies and their products forge new spaces, times, and preferred practices for learning that occurs both in and outside the classroom (Mirra, 2018; Rowsell et al., 2017; Thomas & Brown, 2011). Therefore, when defining technology integration, multiple learning frameworks lend themselves to the if, how, when, and why of teaching and learning practices that technology affects.

A Short History of the Teaching of English and Technology Integration

Prior to Pasternak et al.'s 2018 nationwide study *Secondary English Teacher Education in the United States*, Smagorinsky and Whiting's 1995 pre-internet study, *How English Teachers Get Taught*—considered the benchmark of English teacher education until 2018—there was little mention of technology and its connection to English language arts education in the syllabi they included in their book as exemplars. Technology knowledge and its impact on the English language arts is not listed as course content in the syllabi analyzed for that study, nor is it listed in any designated readings. Student requirements were submitted as papers, sometimes typed with carbon copies, but there are no instructions to submit assignments using word processing, spell checking, or online resources. Despite at least one syllabus specifying a requirement that microteaching be videotaped for self-evaluation and reflection, there was no evidence that technology was taught in English teacher education or might affect how the English language arts were studied. In the 1990s, the phenomenon of integrating technology into the English language arts, as well as other disciplines, was just emerging (Landry & Stewart, 2005).[1]

By 1997, though, the National Council for Accreditation of Teacher Education (NCATE), the organization that pre-dates the Council for the Accreditation of Teacher Preparation (CAEP) and an organization that has partnered with the National Council of Teachers of English in certifying many teacher education programs in the US, reported a need to integrate technology into teaching practices. At that time, NCATE's task force on Technology and the New Professional Teacher reported:

> Perhaps the best way the faculty can inspire teachers-in-training to use technology is to cast themselves as learners and to experiment fearlessly in the application of technology. The teacher education faculty can make themselves role models of lifelong learning if they create for themselves situations in which they must learn from each other and from their students.
>
> (NCATE, 1997, p. 17)

The NCATE report warned teacher educators not to "treat technology as a special addition to the teacher education curriculum" (1997, p. 13), but use technology as practice, not practice technology. Kinzer and Leander (2003) echoed this concern when they called for "technology as practice (rather than simply material 'tool')" (p. 550). Since the 1990s, scholarship in English teacher education has detailed criteria to treat technology as pedagogical content knowledge (Jonassen, Howland, Moore, & Marra, 2005; Pope & Golub, 2000; Yagelski, 2005; Young & Bush, 2004), providing guidelines for integrating technology into the methods (teaching) classroom that reflect real-world applications instead of "as a tool to learn traditional [English language arts] skills and materials" (Swenson, Young, McGrail, Rozema, & Whitin, 2006, p. 163). Scholars have noted the evolving nature of English education considering how technology has created new literacy practices:

> An examination of literacy practices involving technologies deserves special attention, not because they are separate, but because they are central to effective English education in a rapidly changing world. As Leu (2005) noted, the Internet as well as other kinds of newer technologies and new literacies afforded by the Internet are literacy issues, not technologies issues, for English and literacy educators.
>
> (Swenson et al., 2006, p. 353)

Starting in the late 1990s then, after Smagorinsky and Whiting published their study, English teacher educators were urged to "treat technology as a . . . topic that needs to be incorporated across the entire teacher education program" (NCATE, 1997, p. 13).

Fast-forward over 20 years, and technology usage has been profound in how it has changed communication practices by altering how we read and what we read (Beach et al., 2010). These changes can be observed by charting revisions to the English language arts content teacher standards. George et al. (2015) observed that technology usage was addressed in nine sub-indicators of effective practice in the 1997 NCTE content teacher standards. By 2012, the standards "saw the integration of contemporary literacies and contemporary technologies on such a regular basis that it seems safe to say that technology has been part of the English language arts discipline itself, not just a tool for teaching and learning" (p. 9). The ability to read and compose multimedia texts may become as foundational to the English language arts as the study of literature, composition, language, and oratory (George et al., 2015) —a statement that echoes Goodwyn's prediction indicated earlier.

Educating English Language Arts Teachers Today

As technology continues to impact modes of communication, English educators are now obligated to educate English language arts teachers to "integrate, infuse, and implement it in [their] classes" (George et al., 2015, p. 9). According to the US Department of Education's Office of Education Technology's Learning Technology Effectiveness report (2014), technology includes *tools* "that enable design, media production, self-expression, research, analysis, communication, collaboration, and computer programming" (p. 3) that allow for the "development of deeper learning skills such as problem solving, critical thinking, and inquiry" (p. 3). These tools include digital and media texts and games; online learning; course management systems; mobile phones, laptops, and tablets; broadband; social media; assessment and testing systems; and many more applications, hardware, and software that affect learning and communication.

At present, most K–16 students will use some type of technology to communicate with instructors, navigate a school's infrastructure, participate in instruction and school communities, and learn a discipline's content knowledge and technology's impact on transforming that knowledge (Gorgina & Hosford, 2008). To be current in the field of English teacher education and address what Ernest Morrell (2015) calls "doing tomorrow in today's classrooms" (p. 312), English language arts teacher educators need to know which new literacies, new media, and technologies integrate effectively into classroom practices so that the future teachers they educate can learn to support their own students to become literate members of a changing society. The pressure to integrate technology into the English language arts, whether it comes from an understanding of changing literacy practices or from outside forces looking to corporatize aspects of education and its assessment (e.g., Pearson or McGraw-Hill products), underscores the need for a critical approach to integrating and teaching technology as English language arts. Therefore, advocates for technology integration (Young & Bush, 2004) have observed from early on that a critical mindset needs to be fostered in English teachers, teacher candidates, and educators to understand the complexity of technology integration and its continuous effect on the field of literacy by recognizing and understanding:

1. The complexity of technology integration and its status in the field.
2. The evolving and continuous effect computer, information, and Internet technology has on literacy.
3. The importance of creating relevant contexts for effective technology integration by

   a. Developing a pedagogical framework.
   b. Asking important questions.
   c. Establishing working guidelines.
   d. Implementing these strategies while integrating technology.
   f. Reflecting on the experience and revisiting these strategies regularly.

(Young & Bush, 2004, p. 1)

Evolving concepts of literacy have been difficult to maintain across teacher education programs and their methods courses in the United States (Pasternak et al., 2016), as well as in teaching practices in other countries teaching English as a first and second language. Goodwyn (Hawthorne et al., 2012) observes that integrating technology into English language arts classes in New Zealand, similar to the United States, occurs inconsistently, because teachers are not confident in their own use of technology. He notes that literacy practices supported through technology do not align well with assessment systems that still focus on traditional print texts, a situation that complicates evaluating students' proficiency with digital texts. Hamilton and colleagues (Hamilton et al., 2015) provide more detail concerning this development when they observe that new literacy practices created through multimodality are marginalized in some educational settings due to similar privileging of print over digital texts, producing a misalignment in assessment practices in Canada, the United Kingdom, Australia, and Sweden.

For example, these types of assessment misalignments can be illustrated by looking at the English teacher Praxis II exam (ETS, 2019), the content knowledge test that many future English language arts teachers must take in the US. The test taker is asked to analyze a literary passage out of context to the entire work and select an analysis or comprehension answer from a list of multiple choices. The test is given online using multiple-choice questioning and does not take advantage of the affordances of technology to replicate the personalized, multiple perspectives valued in literary analysis that has traditionally been provided through other means.

Additionally, machine scoring of writing has been called into question, because:

> Computers are unable to recognize or judge those elements that we most associate with good writing (logic, clarity, accuracy, ideas relevant to a specific topic, innovative style, effective appeals to audience, different forms of organization, types of persuasion, quality of evidence, humor or irony, and effective uses of repetition, to name just a few). Using computers to "read" and evaluate students' writing (1) denies students the chance to have anything but limited features recognized in their writing; and (2) compels teachers to ignore what is most important in writing instruction in order to teach what is least important.
>
> (NCTE, 2013)

Moving mandatory assessments to digital environments places pressures on students, school districts, and universities to provide the expensive hardware, software, and broadband that might not normally have been purchased. Thus, the testing environment may become such a high-priced item that the entity cannot purchase the best assessment product to run on it. Under conditions such as these, it should not be unexpected that English teacher educators and their teacher candidates in the United States, as well as in other countries, experience tension while learning to integrate technology and new literacies into effective teaching practices in support of what former NCTE president Ernest Morrell (2015) calls doing tomorrow in today's schools to address the needs of a changing, literate society. Those advocating for technology integration under the connected learning model (Ito et al., 2013) explain that "technology tools are not valuable in and of themselves, but to the extent that they" bring together the various community, school, and home stakeholders that support student learning (Mirra, 2019, p. 267). Advocates argue that connected learning offers a vision of technology integration that sees the power in the social practices created through technology, an approach to technology integration that undergirds its usage with a pedagogical vision in support of the practices being integrated.

The teaching of multimodal literacies and technology integration into classroom practice have become integral aspects of the discipline that demonstrate how complex it has become. Both hardware and software, and their products, have changed literacy practices (Conference on English Education [CEE] Executive Committee, 2008)—changes that have affected the content of the English language arts as well as its delivery. These changes can be seen in much of the scholarship that explores the complexities of technology's effect on communication practices—effects that started in the late 1990s.

The journal *Research in the Teaching of English's* "Annual Annotated Bibliography" listings of technology related scholarship underscore the complexity of teaching English in a multimodal world. Originally published annually in print, the bibliography has expanded from 15 pages in 2003 to its most current version (2019) of 43 pages (in 2010, the bibliography grew to an expansive 88 pages). The breadth of the bibliography has required the journal to exclusively publish online. Its size has much to do with the increased numbers of studies that explore technology's impact on the teaching of English (Beach et al., 2010), articles which provide commentary, principles, frameworks, and practices to achieve effective technology integration into the English language arts. Notwithstanding the abundance of studies that address technology and it effect on all the diverse areas of English content, studies rarely consider how technology is integrated into the English language arts methods course and/or across programs to educate future teachers of English (Pasternak, Caughlan, Hallman, Renzi, & Rush, 2014) and/or the English teacher educators who instruct this content. Nelson, Voithofer, and Cheng (2019) observe "While a wealth of research focuses on preservice teachers (Kay, 2006), little emphasis is placed on teacher educators, who are a largely understudied group" (p. 332).

Principles and Frameworks in the Integration of Technology Into the English Language Arts

Pope and Golub (2000) proposed a set of principles and practices for integrating technology into English language arts classrooms, specifically in the methods classroom, the class considered the central location where teacher candidates develop their subject-matter-specific pedagogical content knowledge (Ball et al., 2008; Shulman, 1987). Pope and Golub (2000) thought the methods classroom was the location to educate future English teachers for the change in instruction that seemed imminent to them. This commentary became significant because it challenged researchers to explore and test the 21st-century literacy practices that were changing communication models and the content of the English language arts classroom (Bruce & Levin, 2003; Kinzer & Leander, 2003; Merkley, Schmidt, & Allen, 2001; Swenson et al., 2006; Yagelski, 2005).

Subsequently, Young and Bush (2004) proposed a critical approach and pedagogical framework to maximize the benefits of technology to teach writing and literacy to discern whether technology was being integrated into a lesson with "thoughtful and informed use" (p. 9), asking users to keep the pedagogical implications of the technology in the forefront as users considered its impact on instruction, skills, content, and literacy. They developed their framework after surveying preservice teachers in methods classes and inservice teachers who were participating in a National Writing Project site. They stressed that the incorporation of technology into learning should consider equity and access, empowerment, transparency, expand literacy skills, and enhance critical learning. They warned that technology should not replace teachers or complicate conventional modes of communication that work well. They especially urged teacher educators to model effective practices of teaching with technology in their methods classes.

In response to this call, I conducted a three-year, mixed-methods longitudinal study (2007) in alignment with the 1997 NCATE report directing English teacher educators to model effective technology integration (Young & Bush, 2004). I conducted my English language arts methods classes in a computer lab and learned that the choices preservice teachers in English made to integrate technology into their practice indicated what they valued about teaching, their comfort with technology, how they conceived and envisioned their content knowledge, and where they found support to engage in experimentation. Teacher candidates' decisions to practice with or without technology resembled the choices made by members of most

English departments, with these decisions reflecting specific teacher values about the discipline and how those values are expressed in practice. Technology use or rejection indicated teacher candidates' comfort with active and/or collaborative learning environments. The ease with which preservice teachers learned a technology that would enhance a lesson communicated dispositions and/or attitudes about teacher candidates' comfort in the classroom, their philosophies about classroom management, their perception of equal access, and their impressions of technology being relevant to real-world experiences.

Similarly, in a five-year longitudinal study that examined work samples and reflective data, Thieman (2008) explored the extent to which preservice teachers integrated technology into their instructional planning after taking a stand-alone educational technology course offered over two semesters. Data were analyzed through the lens of the National Educational Technology Standards and Performance Standards for Teachers (NETS-T) and National Educational Technology Standards for Students (NETS-S), as designed by the International Society for Technology in Education (ISTE, 2000/2019). Thieman learned that 85% of the preservice teachers who participated in the study integrated technology into their instructional design to some varying degree, often dependent on grade level. Findings indicated that technology was used to emphasize "creativity and innovation, communication and collaboration, and research and information fluency. There was little evidence that students used technology in other areas . . . including critical thinking, problem solving, and decision-making" (Thieman, 2008, p. 362).

In a case study examining teacher candidates' teaching and learning in a New and Multimodal Literacies class organized under the connected learning model (Ito et al., 2013) Mirra (2019) explained,

> I strove to offer students connected learning experiences to counter the magical views of technology that have proliferated across the educational landscape and instead put the focus back on literacy pedagogy that is relevant, engaging, and transformative for young people.
>
> (p. 285)

Despite some frustrating moments to engage with technology, she felt her six graduate students "were beginning to conceptualize literacy as a social practice and literacy teaching as a means to empowering young people across the overlapping spheres of their lives" (p.285) in this elective course. However, her findings did support that the connected learning framework under which her study took place needed complementary content under a connected teaching framework to support her teacher candidates through the "expanded vision of literacy" (p. 286) her study built upon.

In a follow-up study to Pasternak (2007), Doerr-Stevens and Pasternak (in review) found that teacher candidates actively engaged technology in powerful, creative ways in a course that had them study the composing process through multimodal text creation. However, once the teacher candidates were in their clinical experiences two semesters later, they could only find usage for technology to present information, manage their classroom environments, and/or provide assessment feedback to their students.

These studies, although they called for the integration of technology into the content of the English language arts classroom and explored how pre- and inservice teachers might effectively do so, did not address the purpose of the methods class where the study took place and how it fit into the broader English education program. It is unclear whether the technology skills and content under examination are infused throughout programs or are offered in one focused technology class, although Mirra (2019) does indicate her study was conducted in an elective course and Doerr-Stevens and Pasternak's study (in review) took place in a course taken prior to the first methods class, where technology integration was modeled. Technology should be integrated throughout the K–12 English language arts curriculum to inform the way people think about texts, language, and literacy (Pasternak et al., 2018; Swenson et al., 2006).

Practices in Technology Integration: Open and Closed Technology

Technology and the teaching of the English language arts can be sorted into two not completely exclusive groupings: *open* and *closed* technology. Technology that *opens* spaces for collaborative learning, such as wikis, blogs, discussion boards, and online tutoring provide spaces for collaboration and supports learner agency and has the "potential to transform education not because of the affordances of any particular tool but because it creates a new ecology of learning that fosters collaboration, communication, and creativity" (Mirra, 2018, p. 1). Mirra's (2018) observation aligns with what Rowsell et al. (2017) call the "knowledge work" (p. 158) associated with technology integration into the English language arts and literacy education. They assert that technology instruction needs to be more than a utilitarian or supplemental tool (Hsieh, 2018), but interdependent with a discipline's content (DeCoito & Richardson, 2018) to position teachers and teacher candidates to move "beyond notions of skills-based competency" (Hsieh, 2018, p. 273)—technology integration that empowers learners and learning (Rowsell et al., 2017).

Technology that acts as a utilitarian or supplemental tool, that appears to "close" spaces to support individualized learning or assess that learning, such as desktop applications, e-portfolios, and some multimodal and multimedia software, falls into the second grouping. This type of technology often acts as a substitute or augmentation to another educational approach but does not modify, redefine, or create new tasks the way *open* technology does (Hsieh, 2018).

Under both groupings of open and closed technology, teacher candidates learn technology to understand the content of the English language arts while their teacher educators assess their ability to "develop proficiency and fluency with the tools of technology" (NCTE, 2013, para. 2). Thus, effective technology integration should not only support the learning of the traditional content of the English language arts (i.e., literature, composition, language, and oratory) but also, under this complex process, become content when the software and/or hardware must be learned to engage the content of the English language arts, becoming interdependent. As mentioned earlier, a significant number of studies looked at these aspects of technology integration but were done out of context to the curriculum and programmatic requirements of English teacher education programs.

Open, Collaborative Learning Spaces: Wikis, Blogs, Discussion Boards, and Online Tutoring

Studies of English language arts methods classes examined the use of Web 2.0 applications to "harness a group's collaborative, creative energy to produce shared knowledge that benefits everyone" (Evans, 2006, as quoted in Matthew, Felvegi, & Callaway, 2009, p. 51). Since most Web 2.0 applications supported collaborative and social environments on the internet, many of these spaces became places outside physical classrooms to provide non-traditional field experiences to preservice teachers. In some programs, technology and new media provided field opportunities to preservice teachers isolated by scheduling problems and inconvenient distances. Some programs created virtual places for online tutoring between teacher candidates and K–12 students in the community, while other teacher education programs used similar spaces for cross-disciplinary and cross-global collaboration (Pasternak, 2007), as well as the more typical place for virtual discussion between face-to-face class meetings.

Matthew et al. (2009), using case-study methodology, examined the use of wikis and how they affected the learning of course content by preservice teachers. Through a wiki, preservice teachers learned an "appreciation of their classmates' knowledge and recognized it as a valuable resource" (Matthew et al., 2009, p. 67), by creating a collective synthesis of knowledge gained in that class with that gained from other courses across their programs.

In another study (Dymoke & Hughes, 2009), a wiki was also used to build collaborative content knowledge about poetry for preservice teachers. The investigators examined their students' abilities to write in a digital medium and how it impacted their perceptions of themselves as writers and teachers of poetry writing. The wiki space became a "new" space to collaborate with preservice teachers from the United Kingdom and Canada to write together. Dymoke and Hughes conclude that this digital collaboration allowed some of the preservice teachers to experiment with poetic forms and reflect on themselves as writers while developing technology skills to various degrees of competence. Unfortunately, by composing in a new space, the original poetry written in the wiki seemed to end in that space and not affect a writer's ability to write more effectively.

Lee and Young (2010) examined how preservice teachers use Web 2.0 technologies (wikis and blogs) in their methods class and how learning these applications affected their preparation. By aligning their findings with six of the models of new literacies identified in Jenkins et al. (as quoted in Lee & Young, 2010), Lee and Young found that incorporating wikis and blogs into their English/Social Studies methods class supported opportunities for collaboration and active learning through a constructivist stance and created a community of practice by "(1) enabling the valuing of multiple ideas in civic contexts; (2) encouraging discourse on emerging ideas; and (3) modelling ways of thinking about new ideas" (2010, Conclusion, Implications section, para. 4).

Lee and Young's (2010) findings align with those from Ryan and Scott's (2008) examination of large-group online discussion forums over a period of six years. Ryan and Scott learned that the most effective way to spark professional discourse among preservice teachers is by employing case-study scenarios that allow teacher candidates to move into the role of "expert" as they develop critical literacy skills. Their findings reinforced that "online environments are democratic in that they allow participants who do not speak in classes an opportunity to have a voice and no one dominates the discussion" (Ryan & Scott, 2008, p. 1639).

Houge and Geier (2009) examined the effectiveness of using videoconferencing for one-on-one tutoring in reading instruction by tracking improvement of the tutees through pre- and post-reading and spelling scores. This experience was an opportunity for university students to apply the skills they acquired in a teaching reading class and for the 4–12th grade students to improve their reading abilities using distance-education technology. Findings suggested that "one-to-one literacy instruction via videoconferencing technology can be an engaging and effective means to assist adolescents with comprehension while reading with appropriate accuracy and fluency" (Houge & Geier, 2009, p. 161).

Similarly, videoconferencing provided an additional space for "traditional" preservice teachers (e.g., Caucasian, middle class) an opportunity to work with urban youth to explore multiliteracies in Garcia and Seglem's study (2013) of digital partnerships. The conferencing and chat room contact allowed the teacher candidates to develop an increased awareness of language usage while engaging in student-teacher relationships that improved student achievement and bridged cultures.

Ortega's study (2013) of digital practices (open and closed) and literacy identities brought together an understanding of literacy, technology, and teaching practices for preservice teachers engaged in a year-long internship. The participants engaged in technology practices divided into "tool-for-result (nonintegrated)" and "tool-and-result" (integrated approaches); findings indicated that understanding stemmed from the program facilitating "ample conditions for some of these engagements . . . inquiry and experimentation, professional collaboration, and practical engagements with multiple kinds of texts and technologies" (p. 316).

Benko, Guise, Earl, and Gill (2016) examine Twitter (Twitter.com) as a space for teacher candidates to not only critically reflect upon their own teaching (closed), but for them to participate in a community of practice (open) with other teachers and teacher candidates. Findings indicated that Twitter was a useful space for these activities but required structured assignments to "best support learning and reflecting" (p. 17).

Moran (2018) studied the use of Slack (www.slack.com) as a digital third space constructed around connected learning principles for teacher candidates and 9th graders to collaborate on video creation. The goal was to improve teacher candidates' self-efficacy with digital literacies and provide support to high school students in multimodal composition. Findings supported digital spaces as field experiences for teacher candidates when in-person experiences are not possible, although all the stakeholders felt the need for in-person contact.

Studies such as these addressed how aspects or specific classes within English teacher education programs have met the changing contexts that technology has imposed on literacy practices, but not on a grand scale. Many of these studies seemed to take place in isolated instances within a program instead of across a program, promoting questions as to how the theoretical and pedagogical approaches taught in a program are affected by this integration and how does it affect the effectiveness of the preservice teachers as they move into their internships.

Closed or Individualized Learning Spaces: Desktop Applications, e-Portfolios, Multimodal, and Multimedia Software

Portfolio assessment has become the standard practice in many teacher education programs to evaluate a teacher candidate's competency (Hochstetler & McBee Orzulak, 2015; Hochstetler & McBee Orzulak, 2019).

These practices are particularly common in the assessment of English content, with many English teacher education programs moving to online portfolios to provide convenient access to large collections of artifacts and data, solving the problem of continuing a means of assessment that has long been valued in the teaching of writing. Despite this convenience, in moving to online portfolios teacher education programs have been challenged to ask their teacher candidates to pay for applications that allow access to program instructors and, in some cases, the state's teacher licensing body. In addition to integrating technology into a methods course and purchasing online portfolio applications, many teacher education programs require some type of instructional technology course that asks teacher candidates to not only explore internet applications but to also become adept at desktop applications and multimedia software like PowerPoint, Movie-Maker or iMovie, WebQuest, Adobe Dreamweaver, and the like.

The use of video to analyze teacher candidates' own teaching practices during student teaching was examined by Schieble, Vetter, and Meacham (2015). This study revealed how teacher candidates consider their teacher identities using discourse analysis and become more aware of their classroom presence to improve student achievement.

Earlier, Seo, Templeton, and Pellegrino (2008) examined the effects of multimedia on project-based learning that affected the content knowledge of preservice teachers. The researchers found that the technology methods employed in a project-based learning course promoted a "learner-centered constructivist model, helps students develop skills for retrieving information from multiple resources and motivates students intrinsically by providing a sense of ownership and accomplishment" (Seo et al., 2008, p. 260), much like many of the studies that explored the integration of Web 2.0 technology. Data revealed that multimedia-assisted, project-based learning contributed to increased content knowledge and improved technology skills for the preservice teachers. Additionally, the subjects formed more sophisticated teaching philosophies though this work, despite some obstacles with the technology and its access.

In a course similarly constructed to Seo et al.'s, McVee, Bailey, and Shanahan (2008) studied how technology integration affected the learning of their pre- and inservice graduate students who were taking a 15-week class on new literacies and technology. This small group of "traditional"-aged university students completed digital projects using internet browsers, PowerPoint, WebQuests, Dreamweaver, iTunes, iMovie and others. Data revealed that teacher educators "must foster environments to share problem-solving and distributed learning, to support design and multimodal redesign of texts, and to explore literacy and technology as transactional processes" (McVee et al., 2008, p. 197), although these situations required support for the teacher candidates to successfully integrate technologies into their practices. The researchers concluded that "the daily decisions that teachers make and the instruction that results from those decisions are often far more important than the technology that teachers use to enact their instruction plans" (McVee et al., 2008, p. 208).

Figg and McCartney (2010) reported on the impact of a community-partnered digital storytelling initiative conducted through the "Amazing Technologists Think Teach and Create Stories of Excellence" (ATTTCSE) Project, a project designed for the second year of a three-year study that explored the integration of writing, technology, and diversity through the Technological Pedagogical Content Knowledge, or TPACK, model of technology-enhanced field experiences. In addition to other subjects and data collection, while enrolled in their university's instructional technology course, the researchers studied how teacher candidates facilitated the project's digital storytelling summer workshops as an alternative to their field experiences. Despite their assertions that they learned more about facilitation than teaching through this experience, the researchers' data analysis concluded that the teacher candidates benefited from this alternative experience. Other studies in digital storytelling (Tendero, 2006), digital video composing (Miller, 2010), and e-reading and writing (Luce-Kapler & Dobson, 2005) and their impact on the competency of teacher candidates proliferate. VoiceThread technology was used by Carlson and Archambault (2013) to support preservice teachers to teach poetry following the TPACK framework. Data revealed that VoiceThread was an effective way to provide multiple representations of poetry. Findings indicate there is a need for educating teacher candidates to understand differences in print and digital media in addition to establishing some level of comfort with the hardware and software that create it.

Lai and Calandra (2010) learned through a study of reflective writing practices that e-portfolios could be used as "computer-based scaffolds to augment reflective practice in technology-enhanced educational systems" (p. 421), findings that also require knowledge of hardware and software to create assessment material that is easily accessible to the teacher educators who will be evaluating it—a situation that requires the development of new skills on many levels.

More recently, Baker-Doyle (2018) grappled with coding as an aspect of critical literacy important to the field. Following connected learning principles, she explored the "relationship between making, coding, and critical literacy in the context of literacy teacher education" (p. 1). She makes the point that coders, in writing software, create a form of media that most people cannot read, limiting our ability to engage in civic discourse and work. She observes that "bridging critical literacies of English and computer code has potential to foster greater civic participation and agency" (p. 266).

Marlatt studied (2019) the use of video to produce stories of introduction to teacher candidates' future students, arguing that this type of technology integration complicates the open and closed technology categorization discussed in this book. In producing video stories that provided opportunities for teacher candidates to examine literacy identity, Marlatt observes that their creation is:

> Situated simultaneously within the reflective, communicative contexts of university spaces as well as practicum classroom settings, literacy story videos are an example of an implementation that could potentially support preservice teachers equally in both open and closed processes. (2019)

Thus, it is worth note that technology integration often crosses back and forth between creating collaborative environments and supporting individual learning experiences. How the technology is integrated into the learning and teaching of English will determine how complex its usage is to make new knowledge.

Many of the studies reviewed in this section did not take place in *the* English language arts methods class, but one designed to explore the competency of using technology for teaching purposes. It is unclear how many of these studies are connected to an English language arts program's curriculum and if these skills, conceptual and practical, are fostered or developed elsewhere in the education of a teacher candidate.

As apparent from the range of studies conducted over the years since NCATE's 1997 call to address technology in the English language arts, the integration of technology into the English language arts instructional practices is an increasingly important area of emphasis that warrants the field's attention.

Overview of the Chapters

In Chapter 2 **Teaching and Learning with Technology: Tensions in the Field**, I provide a discussion of the tensions encountered by English teacher educators as they attempt to integrate technology into their methods courses and across their programs as drawn from the national study of English language arts methods courses (Pasternak et al., 2018). This chapter outlines/ overviews the national study from which the data for this book is drawn. Then it identifies the challenges met in the integration process as indicated in Chapter 1: finding expertise in not only the teaching of English language arts but also in technology platforms and applications, accommodating the unequal funding among universities and school districts and between school districts for field placements, the struggle between distracted and engaged students when using technology in the English language arts classroom, the inconsistencies of technology policies, the use of standards for effective integration, and the corporatization of technology in education. It concludes with a case study of a course that has integrated technology throughout its English teacher education curriculum.

In Chapter 3: **Integrating Technology to Learn English Language Arts Methods,** I discuss which open and closed technologies teacher educators ask their teacher candidates to employ in their own learning in the methods course, answering the question, "Which technologies do teacher candidates need to know to learn the content of English language arts methods?" The chapter includes case studies of three courses that employ technology in the teaching of the English language arts methods. Additionally, it draws upon the study's finding more specifically learned from the syllabi and focus group discussions.

In Chapter 4: **Integrating Technology to Teach English,** I discuss which open and closed technologies teacher candidates incorporate into their own lessons to teach English, answering the question, "Which technologies do teacher candidates incorporate into their own teaching practices?" This chapter includes case studies of six courses that require teacher candidates to integrate some type of technology into their English language arts content lessons. It draws specifically on the findings learned from the syllabi and focus group discussions.

In Chapter 5: **Complicating the Teaching of English: Technology and its Integration,** looking across all phases of the national study, I discuss how technology integration has changed the content of the English language arts, who uses it, and to what extent it has affected the teaching of English, which practices transfer into teacher candidates' classrooms, and who is driving its value. As technology changes the field's understanding of content in the English language arts classroom, this chapter explores its consistency of use and its promotion as a panacea for education (US DOE, 2016).

In **Appendix: A Brief Discussion of Research Design,** I provide a description of the methods used to collect and analyze data for the national study. This information is placed in an appendix so that readers may engage immediately with the content of the book. Some readers will want to read the appendix first before moving on to the chapters.

Note

1. However, it is interesting to note that when I certified to teach in 1976, my program required a class in audio-visual equipment management that included the

skills to thread a movie, splice film, and run a mimeograph machine. This class was an additional class taught outside the methods class even then. Furthermore, all teacher candidates in my program were videotaped to reflect upon our classroom presence.

References

Baker-Doyle, K. J. (2018). I, pseudocoder: Reflections of a literacy teacher-educator on teaching coding as critical literacy. *Contemporary Issues in Technology and Teacher Education, 18*(2), 255–270. Retrieved from www.citejournal.org/volume-18/issue-2-18/english-language-arts/i-pseudocoder-reflections-of-a-literacy-teacher-educator-on-teaching-coding-as-critical-literacy

Ball, D. L., Thames, M. H., & Phelps, G. (2008). Content knowledge for teaching: What makes it special? *Journal of Teacher Education, 59*, 389–407.

Beach, R., Brendler, B., Dillon, D., Dockter, J., Ernst, S., Frederick, A., . . . Janssen, T. (2010). Annual annotated bibliography of research in the teaching of English. *Research in the Teaching of English, 45*(2), AB1–AB88. Retrieved from www.ncte.org/library/NCTEFiles/Resources/Journals/RTE/0452-nov2010/RTE-0452Annotated.pdf

Benko, S. L., Guise, M., Earl, C. E., & Gill, W. (2016). More than social media: Using Twitter with preservice teachers as a means of reflection and engagement in communities of practice. *Contemporary Issues in Technology and Teacher Education, 16*(1). Retrieved from www.citejournal.org/volume-16/issue-1-16/english-language-arts/more-than-social-media-using-twitter-with-preservice-teachers-as-a-means-of-reflection-and-engagement-in-communities-of-practice

Bruce, B., & Levin, J. (2003). Roles for new technologies in language arts: Inquiry, communication, construction, and expression. In J. Flood, D. Lapp, J. R. Squire, and J. M. Jensen (Eds.), *Handbook of research on teaching the English language arts* (pp. 649–657). Mahwah, NJ: Lawrence Erlbaum Associates.

Carlson, D. L., & Archambault, L. (2013). Technological pedagogical content knowledge and teaching poetry: Preparing pre-service teachers to integrate content with VoiceThread technology. *Teacher Education and Practice, 26*(1), 117–142.

CEE Executive Committee. (2008). Beliefs about technology and the preparation of English teachers. *CEE Position Statement.* Retrieved from www.ncte.org/cee/positions/beliefsontechnology

DeCoito, I., & Richardson, T. (2018). Teachers and technology: Present practice and future directions. *Contemporary Issues in Technology and Teacher Education, 18*(2). Retrieved from www.citejournal.org/volume-18/issue-2-18/science/teachers-and-technology-present-practice-and-future-directions

Dixon, J. (1967). *Growth through English.* Champaign, IL: National Council of Teachers of English.

Doerr-Stevens, C., & Pasternak, D. L. (in review). Knowledge work or utilitarian tool? Leveling up the commitment to integrating technology in preservice English teacher education.

Dymoke, S., & Hughes, J. (2009). Using a poetry wiki: How can the medium support pre-service teachers of English in their professional learning about writing poetry and teaching poetry writing in a digital age? *English Teaching: Practice and Critique, 8*(3), 91–106.

Educational Testing Service (ETS). (2019). *Preparation Materials.* Retrieved from www.ets.org/praxis/prepare/materials/5038

Ertmer, P. A. (2005). Teacher pedagogical beliefs: The final frontier in our quest for technology integration? *Educational Technology Research and Development, 53*(4), 25–39.

Figg, C., & McCartney, R. (2010). Impacting academic achievement with student learners teaching digital storytelling to others: The ATTTCSE digital video project. *Contemporary Issues in Technology and Teacher Education, 10*(1). Retrieved from www.citejournal.org/vol10/iss1/languagearts/article3.cfm

Garcia, A., & Seglem, R. (2013). "That is dope no lie": Supporting adolescent literacy practices through digital partnerships. In P. J. Dunston, S. K. Fullerton, C. C. Bates, P. M. Stecker, M. W. Cole, A. H. Hall, D. Herro, & K. H. Headley (Eds.), *62nd yearbook of the literacy research association* (pp. 186–198). Altamonte Springs, FL: Literacy Research Association.

George, M., Pope, C., & Reid, L. (2015). Contemporary literacies and technologies in English language arts teacher education: Shift happens! *Contemporary Issues in Technology and Teacher Education, 15*(1), 1–13. Retrieved from www.citejournal.org/vol15/iss1/languagearts/article1.cfm

Goodwyn, A. (2012). English at the crossroads in England? In Hawthorne, S., Goodwyn, A., George, M., Reid, L. & Shoffner, M. Extending the conversation: The state of English education: Considering possibilities in troubled times. *English Education, 44*(3), 288–311.

Gorder, L. M. (2008). A study of teacher perceptions of instructional technology integration in the classroom. *Delta Pi Epsilon Journal, 50*(2), 63–76.

Gorgina, D., & Hosford, C. (2008). Higher education faculty perceptions on technology integration and training. *Teaching and Teacher Education, 25*(5), 690–696

Guzman, A., & Nussbaum, M. (2009). Teaching competencies for technology integration in the classroom. *Journal of Computer Assisted Learning, 25*(5), 453–469.

Hamilton, H. L., Hydon, R., Hibbert, K., & Stooke, R. (2015). *Negotiating spaces for literacy learning: Multimodality and governmentality.* London, UK: Bloomsbury.

Harris, J., Mishra, P., & Koehler, M. (2009). Teachers' technological pedagogical content knowledge and learning activity types: Curriculum-based technology integration reframed. *Journal of Research on Technology in Education (International Society for Technology in Education), 41*(4), 393–416.

Hawthorne, S., Goodwyn, A., George, M., Reid, L., & Shoffner, M. (2012). Extending the conversation: The state of English education: Considering possibilities in troubled times. *English Education, 44*(3), 288–311.

Hochstetler, S., & McBee Orzulak, M. J. (2015). Moving writing out of the margins in edTPA: "Academic language" in writing teacher education. *Teaching/Writing: The Journal of Writing Teacher Education, 4*(2), Article 5. Retrieved from http://scholarworks.wmich.edu/wte/vol4/iss2/5

Hochstetler, S., & McBee Orzulak, M. J. (2019). Writing problems and promises in standardized teacher performance assessment. In H. L. Hallman, K.

Pastore-Capuana, & D. L. Pasternak (Eds.), *Possibilities, challenges, and changes in English teacher education today: Exploring identity and professionalization* (pp. 58–69). Lanham, MD: Rowman & Littlefield.

Hook, J. N. (1962). The emerging English curriculum: Project English. *The American Behavioral Scientist (Pre-1986)*, *6*(3), November, 35–40.

Houge, T. T., & Geier, C. (2009). Delivering one-to-one tutoring in literacy via videoconferencing. *Journal of Adolescent and Adult Literacy*, *53*, 154–163.

Hsieh, B. (2018). This is how we do it: Authentic and strategic technology use by novice English teachers. *Contemporary Issues in Technology and Teacher Education*, *18*(2), 271–288.

International Society for Technology in Education (ISTE). (2000/2019). *Standards*. Retrieved from www.iste.org/standards

Ito, M., Gutierrez, K., Livingstone, S., Penuel, B., Rhodes, J., Salen, K . . . . & Watkins, S. C. (2013). *Connected learning: An agenda for research and design*. Irvine, CA: Digital Media and Learning Research Hub.

Jonassen, D. H., Howland, J. L., Moore, J. L., & Marra, R. M. (2005). *Learning to solve problems with technology: A constructivist perspective*. Upper Saddle River, NJ: Merrill Prentice Hall.

Kinzer, C. K., & Leander, K. (2003). Technology and the language arts: Implications of an expanded definition of literacy. In J. Flood, D. Lapp, J. R. Squire, and J. M. Jensen (Eds.), *Handbook of research on teaching the English language arts* (pp. 546–565). Mahwah, NJ: Lawrence Erlbaum Associates.

Lai, G., & Calandra, B. (2010). Examining the effects of computer-based scaffolds on novice teachers' reflective journal writing. *Educational Technology Research and Development*, *58*, 421–437.

Landry, S. G., & Stewart, H. (2005). Mobile computing at Seton Hall University: Using technology to increase learning effectiveness. In J. E. Groccia and J. E. Miller (Eds.), *On becoming a productive university: Strategies for reducing cost and increasing quality in higher education*. San Francisco, CA: Jossey-Bass.

Lee, J., & Young, C. (2010). Building wikis and blogs: Pre-service teacher experiences with web-based collaborative technologies in an interdisciplinary method course. *Then Journal*, *287*. Retrieved from http://thenjournal.org/feature/287/

Luce-Kapler, R., & Dobson, T. (2005). In search of a story: Reading and writing e-literature. *Reading Online*, *8*(6). Retrieved from www.readingonline.org/articles/luce-kapler/

Marlatt, R. (2019). This is my story: Preservice English teachers create welcome videos to navigate the places and spaces of their literacy lives. *Contemporary Issues in Technology & Teacher Education*, *19*(2). Retrieved from www.citejournal.org/volume-19/issue-2-19/english-language-arts/this-is-my-story-preservice-english-teachers-create-welcome-videos-to-navigate-the-places-and-spaces-of-their-literacy-lives

Matthew, K. I., Felvegi, E., & Callaway, R. A. (2009). Wiki as a collaborative learning tool in a language arts methods class. *Journal of Research on Technology in Education*, *42*(1), 51–72.

McVee, M. B., Bailey, N. M., & Shanahan, L. E. (2008). Teachers and teacher educators learning from new literacies and new technologies. *Teaching Education*, *19*(3), 197–210.

Merkley, D., Schmidt, D., & Allen, G. (2001). Addressing the English language arts technology standard in a secondary reading methodology course. *Journal of Adolescent & Adult Literary, 45,* 220–231.

Miller, S. M. (2010). Reframing multimodal composing for student learning: Lessons on purpose from the Buffalo DV project. *Contemporary Issues in Technology and Teacher Education, 10*(2).

Mirra, N. (2018, July 3). Connected learning and 21st century English teacher education [Blog post]. *Educator Innovator*. Retrieved from https://educatorinnovator. org/connected-learning-and-21st-century-english-teacher-education

Mirra, N. (2019). From connected learning to connected teaching: Reimagining digital literacy pedagogy in English teacher education. *English Education, 51*(3), April, 261–291.

Moje, E. (2008). Foregrounding the disciplines in secondary literacy teaching and learning: A call for change. *Journal of Adolescent and Adult Literacy, 52*(2), 96–107.

Moran, C. M. (2018). Learners without borders: Connected learning in a digital third space. *Contemporary Issues in Technology and Teacher Education, 18*(2). Retrieved from www.citejournal.org/volume-18/issue-2-18/english-language-arts/learners-without-borders-connected-learning-in-a-digital-third-space

Morrell, E. (2015). The 2014 NCTE presidential address: Powerful English at NCTE yesterday, today, and tomorrow: Toward the next movement. *Research in the Teaching of English, 49*(3), 307–327.

National Council for Accreditation of Teacher Education (NCATE). (1997). *Technology and the new professional teacher: Preparing for the 21st century classroom.* Retrieved from https://eric.ed.gov/?id=ED412201

National Council of Teachers of English (NCTE). (2013). The NCTE definition of 21st century literacies. *NCTE Position Statements*. Retrieved from www2.ncte. org/statement/21stcentdefinition/

National Council of Teachers of English (NCTE). (2013). The NCTE position statement on machine scoring. *NCTE Position Statements*. Retrieved from www2.ncte. org/statement/machine_scoring/

Nelson, M. J., Voithofer, R., & Cheng, S. (2019). Mediating factors that influence the technology integration practices of teacher educators. *Computers & Education, 128,* 330–344.

Ortega, L. (2013). Digital practices and literacy identities: Pre-service teachers negotiating contradictory discourses of innovation. *Contemporary Issues in Technology and Teacher Education, 13*(4), 285–324. Retrieved from www.citejournal. org/vol13/iss4/languagearts/article1.cfm

Pasternak, D. L. (2007). Is technology used as practice? A survey analysis of pre-service English teachers' perceptions and classroom practices. *Contemporary Issues in Technology and Teacher Education* [Online serial], *7*(3), 140–157. Retrieved from www.citejournal.org/volume-7/issue-3-07/english-language-arts/ is-technology-used-as-practice-a-survey-analysis-of-pre-service-english-teachers-perceptions-and-classroom-practices

Pasternak, D. L., Caughlan, S., Hallman, H., Renzi, L., & Rush, L. (2014). Teaching English language arts methods in the United States: A review of the research.

Review of Education, 2(2), 146–185.Retrieved from https://onlinelibrary.wiley. com/toc/20496613/2014/2/2

Pasternak, D. L., Caughlan, S., Hallman, H., Renzi, L., & Rush, L. (2018). *Secondary English teacher education in the United States.* Reinventing Teacher Education Series. London, UK: Bloomsbury Academic.

Pasternak, D. L., Hallman, H. L., Caughlan, S., Renzi, L., Rush, L. S., & Meineke, H. (2016). Learning and teaching technology in English teacher education: Findings from a national study. *Contemporary Issues in Technology & Teacher Education, 16*(1), 373–387. Retrieved from www.citejournal.org/volume-16/ issue-4-16/english-language-arts/learning-and-teaching-technology-in-english-teacher-education-findings-from-a-national-study

Pierson, M. E. (2001). Technology integration practice as a function of pedagogical expertise. *Journal of Research on Computing in Education, 33*(4), 413.

Pope, C., & Golub, J. N. (2000). Preparing tomorrow's English language arts teachers today: Principles and practices for infusing technology. *Contemporary Issues in Technology and Teacher Education* [Online serial], *1*(1). Retrieved from www. citejournal.org/vol1/iss1/currentissues/english/article1.htm

Randel, W. (1958). English as a discipline. *College English, 19*(8), 359–361.

Rowsell, J., Morrell, E., & Alvermann, D. E. (2017). Confronting the digital divide: Debunking brave new world discourses. *The Reading Teacher, 71*(2), 157–165. doi:10.1002/trtr.1603

Ryan, J., & Scott, A. (2008). Integrating technology into teacher education: How online discussion can be used to develop informed and critical literacy teachers. *Teaching and Teacher Education, 24*(6), 1635–1644.

Schieble, M., Vetter, A., & Meacham, M. (2015). A discourse analytic approach to video analysis of teaching: Aligning desired identities with practice. *Journal of Teacher Education, 66*, 245–260.

Seo, K. K., Templeton, R., & Pellegrino, D. (2008). Creating a ripple effect: Incorporating multimedia-assisted project-based learning in teacher education. *Theory into Practice, 47*, 259–265. doi:10.1080/00405840802154062

Shulman, L. S. (1987). Knowledge and teaching: Foundations of the new reform. *Harvard Educational Review, 57*, 1–22.

Smagorinsky, P. (2015). Disciplinary literacy in the English language arts. *Journal of Adolescent and Adult Literacy, 59*(2), September/October, 141–146.

Smagorinsky, P., & Whiting, M. (1995). *How English teachers get taught: Methods of teaching the methods class.* Urbana, IL: Conference on English Education and National Council of Teachers of English.

Swenson, J., Young, C. A., McGrail, E., Rozema, R., & Whitin, P. (2006). Extending the conversation: New technologies, new literacies, and English education. *English Education, 38*, 351–369.

Tendero, A. (2006). Facing versions of the self: The effects of digital storytelling on English education. *Contemporary Issues in Technology and Teacher Education, 6*(2), 174–194. Retrieved from www.citejournal.org/vol6/iss2/languagearts/ article2.cfm

Thieman, G. Y. (2008). Using technology as a tool for learning and developing 21st century citizenship skills: An examination of the NETS and technology use by preserve teachers with their K-12 students. *Contemporary Issues in Technology and Teacher Education*, *8*(4), 342–366. Retrieved from www.citejournal. org/volume-8/issue-4-08/social-studies/using-technology-as-a-tool-for-learning-and-developing-21st-century-citizenship-skills-an-examination-of-the-nets-and-technology-use-by-pre-service-teachers-with-their-k-12-students/

Thomas, D., & Brown, J. S. (2011). *A new culture of learning*. Charleston, SC: Create Space.

United State Department of Education. (2016). *US Department of Education's "Advancing Educational Technology in Teacher Preparation: Policy Brief"*. Retrieved from https://tech.ed.gov/teacherprep/

United States Department of Education, Office of Educational Technology. (2014). *Learning Technology Effectiveness*. Retrieved from https://tech.cd.gov

United States Department of Education, Office of Educational Technology. (2016). Future ready learning: Reimagining the role of technology in education. *2016 National Technology Plan*. US Department of Education. Retrieved from http://tech.ed.gov.

Wilson, A. A. (2011). A social semiotics framework for conceptualizing content area literacies. *Journal of Adolescent & Adult Literacy*, *54*, 435–444. doi:10.1598/JAAL.54.6.5

Yagelski, R. (2005). *Computers, Literacy and Being: Teaching with Technology for a Sustainable Future*. Retrieved from www.albany.edu/faculty/rpy95/webtext/

Young, C. A., & Bush, J. (2004). Teaching the English language arts with technology: A critical approach and pedagogical framework. *Contemporary Issues in Technology and Teacher Education* [Online serial], *4*(1), 1–22. Retrieved from www.citejournal.org/volume-4/issue-1-04/english-language-arts/teaching-the-english-language-arts-with-technology-a-critical-approach-and-pedagogical-framework

2   Teaching and Learning With Technology

Tensions in the Field[1]

Pasternak, Caughlan, Hallman, Renzi, and Rush (2018) studied how content-specific English language arts methods (pedagogy) are taught in English language arts teacher education programs across the United States. This large survey of English teacher education included a nationally distributed, self-administered, online questionnaire. The questionnaire was distributed to teacher educators by the National Council of Teachers of English; respondents were selected because they were identified on websites as English teacher education program directors or methods course instructors. The questionnaire gathered responses to 90 questions that were a mixture of fixed (multiple-choice), partially structured, and open-ended items, some of which were randomly distributed to the respondents so that people were not responding to all 90 questions. The questionnaire was designed to collect general data on English education programs, methods courses, and on programmatic responses to change. At the conclusion of the questionnaire, respondents had the option to voluntarily submit their methods course syllabi for analyses. Respondents who submitted syllabi were invited to participate in focus group interviews.[2]

The study focused on how English teacher educators viewed recent changes in English teacher education and how these changes affected their work. In addition to the general data learned about program sizes, number of credits, teaching expertise, certification levels, methods course content, and clinical experience varieties, the study mapped changes in five focal areas: the intersection between methods courses and field experiences, standards and assessment, integrating reading and writing, teaching diverse learners, and integrating technology into the English language arts.

The study's focus was situated in the English language arts methods course, because this class has been identified as the location in a teacher education program where "teacher candidates develop knowledge of content for teaching, student development and misconceptions specific to the disciplines, and means of representing core concepts" (Pasternak et al., 2018, p. 25). Thus,

> The methods course in English teacher education programs bears the key responsibility of helping teacher candidates address current issues in ELA and classroom contexts. The English methods course is where teacher candidates take the content they have learned about literature, linguistics, writing, etc., and turn the focus of that content on the teaching of secondary students.
>
> (Pasternak et al., 2018, p. 26)

Moreover, the study collected data about the five focal areas from the syllabi collected as part of the survey, the open-ended questions from the questionnaire, and the focus group interviews. The aim of the overall study in its data collection and analysis methods was (a) to provide a current portrait of English teacher preparation, both at the level of the methods course(s) taken by teacher candidates and at the level of the program within which these courses were housed; and (b) to trace the changes in concept and practice that have taken place in English teacher education programs since 1995. This book discusses the findings from the various stages of the study that focus on how English teacher educators address the integration of technology and new literacies in the context of the English language arts methods class and/or across an English teacher education program.

Technology: Essential *Other* Content in ELA Teaching

Findings from the study confirmed that English teacher educators in the United States identified the integration of technology into the teaching and learning of English as essential *other* content that required explicit discipline-based instruction in teacher education programs. As one teacher educator noted in an open-ended questionnaire response,

> [Teacher candidates] should begin to understand how these tools [i.e., technology] enhance learning, and how they change the way students learn. They should have many and multiple opportunities to experiment and play with these technologies, and begin incorporating them into their written and field preparation.

Throughout the findings from the questionnaire, there was acknowledgement as to the importance of technology to changing communication practices. One respondent wrote, "My understanding is that we cannot fully address ELA [the English language arts] without acknowledging that we engage with language through various technologies, and that technological advances drive the development of language in all its uses. Integration is not optional." However, another respondent noted,

> We need to do more with technology [in my specific program] and students are somewhat familiar with how to use technology as college students yet not as K-12 teachers. Seeing more current practices in local schools that address teaching ELA with technology would be helpful. It seems that ELA, as a discipline, is still acceptable as being taught somewhat "technology free" at the middle/ high school level.

Conversely, there were concerns it was the teaching of traditional content and teaching philosophies that needed to be taught to future teachers, not technology that was identified as "tools." When asked how technology integration should be taught in the English language arts methods class, a questionnaire respondent indicated, "Thoroughly, but the center is always the teacher. Technology is not a substitute for solid teaching. It is a support." This warning was echoed in other responses as well.

> Integration of technology should be a means to an end rather than an end in itself. That is, the proper role of technology in an ELA methods course is to support the teaching of English content standards.

Hence, despite the varied reactions to the importance of integrating technology into the teaching of the English language arts, teacher educators did feel it was essential *other* content that had a place in the methods class but not necessarily in their specific curriculum area to teach it. However, when questioned as to where explicit instruction occurred in an English teacher education program, nearly half the respondents indicated that technology was integrated across a program in its coursework (see Table 2.1) as opposed to delivered in standalone courses or solely in the English language arts methods class. One questionnaire respondent stated, "We assume that [teacher candidates] are integrating technology into all their coursework in the major, so we don't have a specific focus on it."

Despite the consensus across the field that technology, multiple literacies, multimodal texts, and digital learning are essential *other* content in English language arts instruction, and that the content has rapidly changed communication practices across the globe and should be taught explicitly in a teacher education program, many respondents indicated that they felt challenged to integrate it meaningfully into their methods courses or across their programs to support teacher candidates (Pasternak et al., 2018) for a number of reasons,

Table 2.1 What is the Primary Means Your Teacher Education Program Uses to Address Rapidly Changing Communication and Information Technology in Teaching and the Workplace?

How addressed	Bachelor's	Post-Bacc	Master's	Alternative
n	174	135	104	24
Not addressed	4.02	4.44	7.69	8.33
Separate course	27.59	26.67	23.08	33.33
Integrated throughout	44.83	46.67	48.08	45.83
Methods course	22.41	19.26	17.31	8.33
Field experiences	1.15	2.96	3.85	4.17

Note. In percentages; missing data omitted.

I think that the Methods courses should be central to addressing the integration of technology (i.e. TPAK). However, I do not feel that students have a strong foundation in the technology (from their [stand-alone] instructional technology courses), and there are many other things to accomplish in methods, so I don't get to do quite as much as I wish.

Tensions, such as the one indicated here, were revealed throughout the study's findings regarding the teaching of technology and its impact on communication practices. These tensions uncover a unique situation for English teacher educators: for English teacher educators to integrate technology effectively into the teaching of English, they must be adept at not only teaching teacher candidates to teach traditional English language arts content (literature, composition, oratory, language, etc.) but they also need to learn and teach the technology applications and platforms that are changing those communication practices for the learning in the methods course and the teaching of the English language arts in each teacher candidate's future classroom. One focus group participant, Joseph Shain (all names are pseudonyms),[3] summarized this situation concisely, "You need to combine your technology with your pedagogy with your content knowledge to create these meaningful moments of instruction for your [teacher candidates]."

A Question of Expertise: Integrating Technology Into English Teacher Education

Generationally, socially, and/or academically, some English teacher educators feel that technology is a distraction in the classroom, obsolete to their own lives, and/or better left to colleagues who are already engaged in it. Conversely, some see their teacher candidates as digital natives who are already adept at understanding technology's impact on communication practices and the content is now irrelevant to the methods course. Dispositions such as these may be easily understood considering how pervasive technology has become to university students trying to earn their degrees or certifications. Even prior to being enrolled in an English language arts methods class, teacher candidates use technology to navigate a university's infrastructure, participate in learning communities through email and other platforms, engage learning through course management systems, word process assignments, and evaluate themselves and their instructors through online assessment instruments. To achieve certification, most teacher candidates will be evaluated for their fitness to teach through high-stakes e-portfolio systems such as Pearson's edTPA (2019). Therefore, it is unsurprising to think that some teacher educators feel technology integration has been learned elsewhere without a discipline-specific use.

Many teacher education programs provide standalone technology courses that are not content-specific or are taught by someone with expertise in technology, but not the discipline's content (Pasternak et al., 2016). In such a situation, Dave Sommer, a focus group participant, indicated, "although we're not directly providing [instruction] within our methods course . . . we're certainly making space for it in our classes." The idea of "making space" for technology integration is echoed in a number of the focus group conversations as well as the open-ended questionnaire responses included earlier.

Alex Terrell, another focus group participant, confirmed that his teacher candidates take a separate technology class but are required to "infuse" the technology learned in that class into the curriculum and lessons they create for their methods class submissions. Similarly, another respondent explained that he assigns a technology-based topic, but it was up to the teacher candidates to find "web-based tools, articles, and videos" to explore its use in English language arts teaching. Despite English teacher educators' awareness that technology integration is important to the discipline, technology integration is sometimes left to the teacher candidates themselves to figure out, a situation that may reflect more on formative teaching philosophies and dispositions than a methods instructor's inability to explicitly instruct this content (Pasternak, 2007; Rust & Cantwell, 2018; Shelton, 2018; Thieman, 2008).

When technology integration is implicitly taught in the ways described earlier, some of the respondents felt its usage was rarely on a critical, actively engaged level. Charles Bates, a focus group participant, observed that his English language arts teacher education program engages in technology teaching and learning,

> But it still primarily means Prezi and PowerPoint. It depends on the rare student, maybe ten percent, that are doing something really creative

or engaging with literacy or a multimodal text. I think that's still very, very slow and something we define as cutting edge or dynamic.

Bates' observation concerning the functional implementation of technology in teaching was echoed by Terrell, whose methods students first take a standalone technology course before the methods class. Once in methods, it becomes the students' responsibilities to find opportunities to integrate technology into their teaching practices, which mostly meant creating presentations or assignments for information gathering. In this situation, Terrell noted, "I don't get the feeling that they're having an opportunity to really fully utilize the technology to the degree that they could."

Similar to the observations expressed by the questionnaire respondents indicated in the previous section, the focus group respondents conveyed having a critical awareness as to the need to integrate technology into the methods class, but felt that teacher candidates' technology choices were often driven by their own and/or by instructor-specific expertise with an isolated application, observations that have been echoed in other scholarship (Rust & Cantwell, 2018; Shelton, 2018).

In counter, some focus group respondents thought technology integration was occurring effectively across their programs. Anita Vogel mentioned that teacher candidates in her program were taking more and more digital literacy and media credits. She said that the program asks teacher candidates to explore literacy by examining its relationship to technology and the choices made in its application, such as in *Schoology* and in voice-over PowerPoints.

> We use it—I think we need to be more thoughtful and consistent about how we do it, but right now we're using a lot of modeling. While we do our normal thing, we're integrating in the technology as a means of expression and response and then reflecting on how that technology changed that activity. That happens in methods, it happens in the general methods course, and it happens in other places throughout the program.

Vogel observes that her program tends to model technology usage to have teacher candidates reflect on its viability. Her response echoes that of an open-ended questionnaire respondent,

> This [technology integration] is an important topic that must be addressed in the ELA methods course by getting teacher candidates to both apply/use technology in lesson planning and implementation and to reflect upon the benefits and drawbacks of reliance on technology in ELA classrooms.

Similar to these concerns, another focus group participant, Caroline Stewart, felt that technology was appropriately integrated throughout the teacher education program in which she works, a joint English Department and School of Education program where technology was infused across coursework, but "not technology for the sake of technology." In Stewart's teacher education program, she felt that technology integration was not high stakes. Rather, like in Vogel's program, it involved modeled practices that fit into a teacher candidate's practice:

> We try to demonstrate [a] kind of seamless incorporation of technology, so not to call attention to using *Skype*, for example, but to use it for what it—what we want it to be used for, like interviews with authors in Adolescent Literature and that kind of thing. So that we're not making it seem difficult to use by calling attention to it. We use, I just have to say, a variety of technologies. Students create weekly websites for their unit plans, for example . . . we try to incorporate technology seamlessly as a tool for greater goals.

Sommer agreed that technology integration in the English language arts generated valuable discussions about its value and use. In particular, he felt that the study of multimodal texts supported teacher candidates to think through a text and not just teach it by having them explore "videos, songs, websites, blogs—a variety of stuff, and really think . . . about how all of these different modes of textuality speak to one another."

Modeling technology use and asking teacher candidates to reflect on its viability was a common integration strategy shared by the teacher educators in the focus group interviews. However, as the data reveals, integrating technology into the English language arts is not an intuitive process and requires time, thought, and practice. Nelson, Voithofer, and Cheng (2019) found that it is more likely for teacher educators to provide explicit technology-integration instruction to their own teacher candidates in the methods classes if they have undergone specific professional development,

> If teacher educators are not provided with the training and resources they need, they may be unable to model appropriate technology usage and demonstrate its value to preservice teachers.
>
> (Nelson et al., 2019, p. 332)

Moreover, Ottenbreit-Leftwich, Ertmer, and Tondeur (2015) have observed that teacher candidates do not adopt technology integration themselves if their teacher educators do not emphasize its use in their methods classes in alignment with the content they will be teaching.

The question of expertise in teaching technology integration across a program or in a methods class is confounded by many opposing opinions. As English teacher educators vary in their conceptions of the teaching of English, often moving into the field for the love of its more traditional content, developing expertise in technology integration may seem like a bothersome add-on if they are not provided with explicit instruction themselves to build expertise.

The Lure of Technology: Distraction or Panacea to Learning

English teacher educators are cautious about the impact of technology on the field. Many articulated recognizing a value in its positive effects on communication practices but also understood that it could be a distraction to the *real* content of the discipline: literature, language, oratory, and composition. Throughout the open-ended questionnaire responses, this concern arose a number of times as indicated earlier. In contrast, a respondent also noted its impact on K–12 student learning, "[Teacher candidates] should begin to understand how these tools enhance learning, and how they change the way students learn." However, in integrating technology into the discipline, teacher educators want to know who provides funding for technology, and, ultimately, who owns it, who promotes it, how it enhances or detracts from the English language arts learning experience, and how it changes the role of the teacher. Sean Prinsen, a focus group participant, explains,

> We had a teacher from a local high school. Her graduate degree is in educational technology. She's super smart and she put together just a wonderful presentation for our student teachers on the use of technology and how she uses it in a . . . public high school. I really loved the presentation, and yet this kind of just enthusiasm for technology—I wanted to have a conversation after that about the assumptions that are underwriting this kind of endorsement of technology. I mean, it's tied to certain, a certain tradition. It's tied to a certain epistemology. It's tied to a certain economic paradigm. I worry about that sometimes.

Prinsen's observations about who funds technology in K–16 schools, from the decision to purchase domain-specific standardized assessment platforms to the dependency on *teacher-proof* computerized lesson modules or reading programs in some districts, challenge what is known about the English language arts and technology integration. Prinsen worries "about the uncritical use of technology," because:

[T]here seems to be so much general enthusiasm for the use of technology in classroom[s] . . . who's supplying this technology? What does this technology imply about the role of the teacher? What costs are—both literal and kind of figurative—are associated with this technology?

Policing Technology

Even though many of the English teacher educators who responded to the study acknowledged the prevalence of technology in education and the importance for teacher candidates to be critically aware of technology's impact on the English language arts, ironically, many university teacher education programs have policies that ban the use of technology during class meeting times. Almost 20% of the syllabi collected for the study articulated technology policies. Eighty-eight percent of those policies banned technology usage in class (Pasternak et al., 2018). Nonetheless, the teacher candidates who have been banned from using technology in their methods class will, ultimately, be assessed on their ability to incorporate technology into their lesson design to satisfy licensing requirements and meet teacher education standards. George, Pope, and Reid (2015) observed that technology usage was addressed in three indicators of effective practice in the National Council of Teachers of English's 1997 teacher standards (NCATE, 1997), and in the most current version of those standards (NCTE/NCATE, 2012) even more emphasis has been placed on contemporary literacies and technologies. Of the seven overarching standards in the 2012 English teacher standards,

> [F]ive have references to contemporary technologies or literacies. In the content knowledge standards, mention is made of multimedia texts, media texts, contemporary technologies, and digital media. Likewise, contemporary technologies/literacies are included in content pedagogy planning standards for reading, literature, and composition, as well as the instructional implementation standards.
>
> (George et al., 2015, n.p.)

Apart from being expected to teach and learn from digital platforms, most teacher candidates are expected to submit materials through course management systems, watch English content-specific videos on YouTube or listen to podcasts, collaborate with K–12 students virtually, and be assessed through e-portfolios (Pasternak et al., 2018). However, many of their methods instructors will not allow them to engage in technology usage during class time per university and/or instructor policy.

Technology policies communicate a tension between technology's value as a teaching and learning device and its detriment to behavior management. One particularly strong policy included in one syllabus, which appears to be a university-wide policy, was typical of some,

> *Cell Phone and Electronic Devices Policy:* Course instructors and staff of [university name] facilities may place restrictions on the use of wireless communication devices and electronic devices in their classroom or facilities. Ringing cellular telephones and laptop computers used for instant messaging, game playing, internet surfing, and other such activities can be considered disruptive. After an initial warning, students who do not comply with the policy of the classroom/facility may be asked to leave for the remainder of the class/day. If students are asked to leave class because of such a disruption, instructors are not obligated to allow makeup of missed work. Having a wireless communication device in hand or using earphones connected to one during examinations also may be grounds for charges of academic dishonesty. Using devices with video or photo features may result in charges of violating laws on intellectual property rights or invasion of privacy.

Technology usage policies such as these reinforce its perceived disruptive nature, sending a mixed message that technology is beyond K–16 classroom management if disruptive to higher education attended by adults. Thus, such technology policies may curtail teacher candidates from learning valuable differentiation strategies. During a focus group discussion, Sommer shared,

> Every classroom, every high school classroom I go into, cell phones are just—they have to be dealt with one way or another. Whether it's getting kids to put them away or getting kids to integrate them into the class—every kid pretty much is carrying around this really powerful pocket computer that's got the answers to information questions all the time.
>
> One of the things I think we have talked about both in terms of classroom management but also in terms of integrating that powerful little computer that kids have—how do we use that in productive ways in a classroom? Even if it's sort of an informal learning tool, how do we allow kids to use that? How do we make sure that there's an equitable distribution when that—the phones are not equitably distributed? All those are questions I think that we do grapple with as well.

Policies that prohibit technology in the methods class may hamper how to manage it for learning, adapt it for equitable distribution, support it as a learning tool, and evaluate it critically for who is supplying it and promoting it for learning—all leading to English teacher educators concerns about its uncritical use for instruction.

Transforming Learning

According to the US Department of Education, Office of Educational Technology's updated report (2017) entitled *Reimagining the Role of Technology in Education: 2017 National Education Technology Plan Update*,

Technology can be a powerful tool for transforming learning. It can help affirm and advance relationships between educators and students, reinvent our approaches to learning and collaboration, shrink longstanding equity and accessibility gaps, and adapt learning experiences to meet the needs of all learners.

Our schools, community colleges, adult learning centers and universities should be incubators of exploration and invention. Educators should be collaborators in learning, seeking new knowledge and constantly acquiring new skills alongside their students. Education leaders should set a vision for creating learning experiences that provide the right tools and supports for all learners to thrive.

However, to realize fully the benefits of technology in our education system and provide authentic learning experiences, educators need to use technology effectively in their practice. Furthermore, education stakeholders should commit to working together to use technology to improve American education. These stakeholders include leaders; teachers, faculty, and other educators; researchers; policymakers; funders; technology developers; community members and organizations; and learners and their families.

(p. 3)

The authors of this report indicated seeing growth in access between the publication of the original report in 2016 and its update in 2017,

In just one year since the release of the 2016 NETP, we have seen rapid change across the country in fundamental aspects of the educational technology landscape. These changes include the number of schools that have access to broadband in their classrooms; the types and cost of technology available to schools; an evolution in the approach of leaders to the procurement of ed tech solutions as well as a greater emphasis on data security and digital citizenship; the advent of new research on the use of technology by early learners; and an increased emphasis on preparing teachers to lead with technology before they arrive in the classroom.

(p. 1)

However, the English teacher educators see an unevenness in access and expressed concern regarding the disproportionate funding, expertise, and use of technology across English teacher education programs and grade schools.

Accessing Technology

Amanda Reiter expressed concern with teaching in a technology-rich university but placing teacher candidates in school districts that were not:

> I really make sure to have that conversation with students [about technology disparities], and also to talk about how do you use technology in the classrooms when you have limited resources. Most of my students teach in schools that are very under-resourced and don't even have very good internet access. We talk about ways to still use technology when you don't have a lot to work with. That can be really challenging, and I've never really had a very good answer for that. Sometimes it's encouraging students to use their own devices or to use their own resources when your school may not have those resources.

Vogel saw the increase in technology integration being driven by the school districts her program partnered with, who put pressure on her teacher education program to provide content they did not have expertise in,

> [T]he school systems are actually driving the increase in digital learning because they're supplying student teachers, for example, with sets of tablets or iPads and saying, "You have to use these. Get going with them. We're going paperless." That's really encouraged us to integrate more and more technology knowledge throughout our program.

Similarly, Sommer expressed concerns about how the high schools he placed teacher candidates in for their clinicals were driving how his program needed to adapt, causing tensions between the program and the field experience as to what content to focus on in methods:

> A lot of the schools that our students go into have Google Drive accounts. Students are using Chromebooks and they're doing a lot of

their writing, the high school students are doing a lot of their writing on Google Docs and sharing those with teachers and getting feedback from teachers that way and doing peer feedback that way. We do some modeling of that just through using Google Docs and Google Drive in our class. That's a technology that when I was teaching I didn't have, so I'm learning that along with them.

Shain agreed with Sommer in feeling a little behind the times when out-resourced by a field placement. As Shain noted earlier in this chapter, for technology to be meaningful content in a methods class, English teachers need to be adept at their English content and pedagogy as well as their technology content and pedagogy. Knowing which technology applications to address in the methods classes can be specific to one field placement but not another. When the technology becomes content to teach content, Shain warned,

> I'm very frustrated because I'm losing class time because I'm teaching technology while I'm teaching a subject area. . . . Because as [Anita Vogel] said, I really feel the school district is driving the teacher educa-tion program. They put their policies in place, they spend a bajillion dollars on this technology, and now I have to teach that technology. Don't get me wrong; we have a very close school district that's referred to as the "corridor of shame" because of the poverty levels down there, and they have—they might have pencils in the classroom.

A tension between programs and school districts manifests in the ineq-uity of the technology available across school districts, and the English teacher education program which may be unable to meet those needs. If the methods class integrates technology appropriate to the most well-funded school district, say, in alignment with the US Department of Education's Office of Educational Technology's 2017 report, teacher educators may be spending their limited methods course time unwisely teaching strategies that will go unused in clinical placements. Study respondents challenged which technology purchases a program can even require of its teacher can-didates. Some respondents felt their programs were able to purchase laptops or require their teacher candidates to do so; other respondents presumed that their teacher candidates have technology or can borrow it from the univer-sity or public library.

Shain was explicit in addressing the tension caused by the unequal resourcing of technology among the university, the program, and the school districts. He felt that English and technology are merged more fluidly in the secondary school classroom and high school students seem to accept its presence more casually than in the lower grades:

> They [teacher candidates] walk into the classroom and they're looking around and all the kids have technology. It quickly hits them that the way they were taught in their college education is not . . . the way they need to teach as a future high school teacher. This really makes them angry. Literally, it makes them angry. I have to put out fires because their expectations don't match the reality and the technology and the infusing of technology into the curriculum is one of these issues. My students either stay angry through their entire internship and they make it through, or they embrace it. I've seen some very great ways that they've done that. . . . You get these cool moments of collaboration, but . . . you have to teach them how to use technology. They have to actually study technology. A standalone course won't work. Teacher-educators who are unsure of how to actually do it then rely on that standalone course, and every time there's technology they might get a couple extra credit points on a rubric, but that's not really reinforcing it. How . . . do I make all that come together?

As evident from these discussions, easy answers are not forthcoming to a profession struggling to define its essential content and find the expertise within it to support future English teachers. The issues described in this section become even more complex in light of the rapid change of technology platforms, devices, and applications and the need to address teacher standards that align to effective English language arts *and* technology instruction.

Standardizing Technology

English educators have historically had an uneasy relationship with standards (Pasternak et al., 2018). Unsurprisingly, standards were never brought up in relation to technology during the focus group interviews. However, over the past 30 years, the updates to English teacher standards have required increased proficiency with technology's effect on communication practices (George et al., 2015). In 2018, the English Language Arts Teacher Educators of the National Council of Teachers of English released an updated belief statement to guide English teacher educators to effectively integrate technology into the English language arts "without abandoning the kinds of practices and principles that we as English educators have come to value and know to work" (NCTE, 2018, n. p.). This belief statement is an updated version of a 2005 document, now offering a layered framework to support colleagues in their efforts to confidently and creatively explore networked, ubiquitous technologies in a way that deepens and expands the core principles of practice that have emerged over the last century in English and literacy education.

Yet, belief statements are not standards to be met by future teachers to show competency, and the field of teacher education sees a need for competencies that cross all disciplines.

As part of the US Department of Education, Office of Educational Technology's updated report (2017) referenced earlier in this chapter, the authors called for technology competencies for all teachers, because:

> Teachers need to leave their teacher preparation programs with a solid understanding of how to use technology to support learning. Effective use of technology is not an optional add-on or a skill that we simply can expect teachers to pick up once they get into the classroom. Teachers need to know how to use technology to realize each state's learning standards from day one.
>
> (p. 35)

This report generated a study (Foulger, Graziano, Schmidt-Crawford, & Slykhuis, 2017) identifying 12 competencies that cross *all* academic disciplines, because:

> Many of the standards or guidelines that influence our work and preparation in teacher education make reference to the use and integration of technology for PK–12 teachers and students, but *there are no technology guidelines that exist specifically for teacher educators to operationalize* [my emphasis] these aforementioned initiatives.
>
> (p. 422)

When I asked respondents which technology standards they addressed in their methods classes, (see Table 2.2) the majority indicated that they asked their students to meet the National Council of Teachers of English technology standards.

In alignment with this finding, Foulger et al. (2017) indicate that professional organizations design their technology content-specific standards to address the knowledge, skills, and dispositions that teacher candidates need to be effective in classrooms,

> But *these standards lack direction and details related to the selection and implementation of content specific technologies* [my emphasis] that are needed for teacher educators.
>
> (p. 421)

Table 2.2 Technology Integration Content Standards Used

Technology standards used in English methods classes: Frequency table (n=146)	
No Technology Standards Taught	35.6
State Teaching Standards	58.9
NCTE/NCATE Teaching Standards	63.7
NCTE 21st-Century Literacies	15.1
NETS-T	23.3
NETS-S	12.3

Note: Values as percent of respondents who chose each option (check all that apply).

These observations lend some credence as to why technology integration may be inconsistently taught throughout many English teacher education programs. Most English teacher educators would follow NCTE or state teaching standards if they are accredited through the Council for the Accreditation of Educator Preparation (CAEP, 2015) or their states. This adherence to professional or state standards may also be an indication that many English teacher educators are unaware of specific technology standards such as ISTE's NETS (2019), TPACK, or connected learning.

As observed throughout the study, expertise in technology integration is a two-step process that requires English educators to be proficient in their field but also in software applications and the devices on which they run. English teacher educators are faced with numerous challenges when integrating technology to meet teacher education standards (NCTE, 2013), some of which might have to do with the lack of specificity found in the guidelines and standards available to them, as well as lack of professional development opportunities.

Actively Engaging Technology for the Teaching and Learning of English

English teacher educators express tension in providing technology integration content to their teacher candidates for both learning in the methods class as well as for incorporating it into their own teaching of English and integrating it into their teaching practices. As evidenced through the questionnaire findings, teacher educators acknowledge an awareness that technology, multiple literacies, multimodal texts, and digital learning are essential *other* content to the discipline of English, especially in terms of its effect on communication practices. To further underscore teacher educators' awareness of technology's impact on the teaching of English, 40% of the respondents indicated that some kind of technology-enhanced content was integrated across their English teacher education programs (see

Table 2.1); however, analysis of the syllabi and the focus group conversations revealed that programs were not consistently teaching technology integration on a critical, actively engaged level (see previous discussions). Data indicate that technology integration was often taught without explicit instruction and, if done so, extended engagement with the technology was generally student- and/or instructor-expertise focused. The syllabi analysis revealed that technology for the teaching and learning of the English language arts was taught at an *awareness* level (see Table 2.3) with only a small number of the syllabi indicating that technology integration occurred at complex or sustained *active engagement* levels (see Table 2.3). Most syllabi indicated that technology integration content was taught at an *awareness* level, asking teacher candidates to engage with it in a passive manner (see Table 2.4).

It is notable to consider that the majority of the questionnaire respondents indicated that technology was integrated across their programs' coursework (see Table 2.1), a finding that was not substantiated in the syllabi analysis. This discrepancy may be due to several factors. Per Pasternak

Table 2.3 Levels of Engagement to Integrating Technology and New Literacies Into the Teaching of ELA Methods

Technology Integration that Guided the Syllabus Analysis

Code	Explanation of Code
1	No mention or evidence that the course addresses the integration of technology in the teaching and learning of the ELA.
2	Awareness or passive engagement. The topic was mentioned in the course description, and/or in the course objectives. The topic may also be mentioned in a calendar topic or set of readings, but there is no evidence of active application other than as a response to course readings. Passive engagement included the writing of technology autobiographies, being told to use a course management system (CMS) or go to a website, or if the CMS was merely a submission system. If technology use was indicated as an option for a lesson, it was coded as passive engagement.
3	Single application or minor active engagement. In addition to readings or discussion of technology, if students were required at least once to address technology in their planning, instruction, or presentation of content, it was coded as minor active engagement. One activity done repeatedly would be coded as minor active engagement.
4	Active engagement. The topic was repeatedly mentioned in course objectives, calendar topics, readings, and assignments (more than one assignment) and activities (blogs, presentation, online tutoring, etc.) Web-based courses were coded as active engagement since the teacher candidates had to use it for learning, but not necessarily teaching.

et al. (2018), about 50% of the English methods courses are taught in English departments, 37% housed in schools or departments of education, with 14% offered jointly between the two. Although these classes are mostly taught by tenure-line faculty, about 25% of the methods classes are taught by part-time instructors and 8% by graduate teaching assistants. The majority of the methods instructors have degrees in English and not education.

Despite over 50% of English teacher education programs being housed in English departments (Pasternak et al., 2018), 8% of syllabi (see Table 2.4) collected for the overall study indicated that active engagement with technology for both teaching and/or learning the teaching of English, 90% of those were for classes housed in schools and colleges of education and not English departments—a finding to consider given the majority of English teacher education programs are housed in English departments, spaces where the teaching of multimodal and multiliteracies would be taught at most universities.

Nonetheless, the response in the questionnaire portion of the study that technology is presumptively thought to be integrated across a program's coursework may be a result of the instructors being unfamiliar with an entire program's structure because the respondent was a part-time employee, graduate student, or instructor housed in departments or schools that were not responsible for providing the rest of the program's content.

When considering the results discussed earlier, it is meaningful to mention that the number of respondents for the overall study of 200 decreased to 175 for the technology portion. The lower number of responses in the technology section may be a result of confusion with the terms *open* and *closed* technology, despite these terms being defined in the questionnaire (and a confusion that did not arise during the piloting of the study); respondents experiencing survey fatigue (Blair, Czaja, & Blair, 2014); or respondents having less knowledge about teaching and learning with technology when

Table 2.4 Program Engagement With Technology Integration Based on Syllabus Analysis

Level	Commitment Explanation	For Learning: n=136	For Teaching: n=136
1	No mention or evidence of topic.	6	9
2	Awareness or passive engagement. Mentioned in standards or objectives.	71	68
3	Minor active engagement. One assignment or activity indicated.	20	18
4	Active engagement. Multiple assignments or activities repeated.	3	5

Note. Values as percent of syllabi collected.

compared to the number of responses in the other content sections of the study (teaching English language learners, integrating reading and writing, addressing standards-based instruction, and aligning field experiences).

In presenting this discrepancy between the questionnaire results and the syllabi analysis, I would be remiss in not mentioning the limitations apparent in using syllabi as a sole source of data (Pasternak et al., 2018) for a study of teacher education. Syllabi are often idiosyncratic documents aligned with an instructor's philosophies of English education or may be formula templates dictated by university policy. Moreover, many university instructors distribute more specific directions in materials supplemental to the syllabus. These more detailed materials may have been distributed in course management systems (CMS) or as paper documents to the teacher candidates, but were not submitted to the researchers as part of the study's request for the respondents to upload methods course syllabi since they may have been thought of as supplemental. Additionally, since many teacher education programs have standalone technology classes taught separately or in addition to the methods class, those syllabi were not submitted as part of the study and could not be analyzed as *methods* courses. Thus, the limitations of syllabi analysis can be illustrated by the widespread reporting in the questionnaire that technology teaching and learning were integrated throughout programs, despite many syllabi giving the impression during analysis that *using a course management system constituted technology integration.* Contrarily, the focus group interviews revealed more robust use of technology to create lessons in the methods classes that were not articulated in the syllabi.

With all this said, only one syllabus submitted for analysis indicated that technology was taught at an *active engagement* level (see Table 2.3) in an English education methods course, requiring multiple assignments or technology activities repeated throughout a semester for *both* teaching and learning the subject of the teaching of English. To create the case for this exemplar of technology integration, I traced the participant's responses through the open-ended sections of the questionnaire and then contacted him to query about his program and methods course for the specifics about technology integration across the program. Finally, he vetted the case I created and confirmed its accuracy (Pasternak et al., 2018). What follows is a discussion of this methods course and how it integrates technology throughout the English teacher education program in which he worked.

Exemplar of Technology Integration for Both the Teaching and Learning of English

As defined previously, technology usage in the study of English should underscore the learning of conceptual knowledge, procedural knowledge, attitudinal knowledge, and/or value-based knowledge specific to that content as a discipline (Guzman & Nussbaum, 2009). Technology should be a tool for learning (Gorder, 2008; Harris, Mishra, & Koehler, 2009) that supports instructional practices (Ertmer, 2005) and is integral to the learning process (Pierson, 2001) but has the "potential to transform education not because of the affordances of any particular tool but because it creates a new ecology of learning that fosters collaboration, communication, and creativity" (Mirra, 2018, p. 1). Or, as Rowsell, Morrell, and Alvermann (2017) suggest, technology usage should be a transformative experience, "knowledge work" (p. 158) that moves past utilitarian or supplemental tool (Hsieh, 2018). Thus, technology integration should *open* spaces for collaboration and support learner agency but, may also *close* some spaces for individualized learning and provide space for more traditional assessment instruments.

Teaching Writing in the Middle and Secondary Schools in the School of Education at Midwestern University (pseudonym) (see Pasternak et al., 2018) exhibited technology usage that moved passed utilitarian and supplemental tool in its thoughtful use of technology in the methods class and how the content taught there was scaffolded across its English teacher education program. Elements of effective technology integration that arose in analysis included the school's early adoption of a 1:1 laptop program to support teacher candidates from their first year of post-secondary education, professional development in technology integration for all program instructional personnel, a Commitment to Technology statement that was clearly indicated in course documents for the teacher candidates to consider, and pre-program acceptance in standalone technology classes that explored changing communication practices in teaching and the workplace, as well as having other classes taught in technology-infused spaces.

The methods class was jointly designed by an English educator and an educational technologist. The syllabus indicated alignment between standards and unit assessment rubrics and its required technology-integration assignments, readings, and communication modes, enabling the teacher candidates to not only navigate their own education at the university, but also explicitly incorporate technology into their own teaching philosophies and practices. The rubric specifies that unit plans will be graded not only on more traditional writing methods content but also articulates that the "Candidate demonstrates the use of a variety of learning skills and technology; demonstrate[s] how each will teach students the safe uses of technology" in alignment with NCTE national standards that were in use at the time the syllabi were collected:

3.6.2 Use a variety of approaches for teaching students how to construct from media and nonprint texts and integrate learning opportunities into classroom experiences that promote composing and responding to such texts; and

3.6.3 Help students compose and respond to film, video, graphic, photographic, audio, and multimedia texts and use current technology to enhance their own learning and reflection on their learning.

The rubric also indicates that "Candidate demonstrates knowledge of teaching various literacies" in alignment with:

3.2.1 Create opportunities and develop strategies that permit students to demonstrate, through their own work, the influence of language and visual images on thinking and composing;

3.2.2 Create opportunities and develop strategies for enabling students to demonstrate how they integrate writing, speaking, and observing in their own learning processes;

3.2.3 Demonstrate a variety of ways to teach students composing processes that result in their creating various forms of oral, visual, and written literacy;

3.2.4 Engage students in activities that provide opportunities for demonstrating their skills in writing, speaking, and creating visual images for a variety of audiences and purposes; and

3.6.1 Understand media's influence on culture and people's actions and communication, reflecting that knowledge not only in their own work but also in their teaching.

Perhaps an ambitious requirement for a three-credit methods class; however, a clear indication to the teacher candidates enrolled in this class that the teacher educator acknowledges the importance of technology integration as part of the field. Likewise, the syllabus indicates the importance of technology to the teacher candidates' own learning by requiring at least one more traditional text that has chapters on new literacies with additional links to various YouTube videos and professional organizations' websites for the teacher candidates to gain access to professional digital resources. Lastly, the teacher candidates submit all their completed assignments into a course management system. The teacher candidates in this class use technology to *open* spaces for collaborative learning alongside *closed* technology that supports their individualized learning or assesses that learning. The teacher candidates use technology to navigate instruction as well as to learn the content of the teaching of English. Technology teaching is integrated across the assignments in alignment with national and state teacher and content standards, directing the teacher candidates to integrate technology into their own writing lessons following guidelines that did not formularize or pinpoint specific applications, but allowed for technology selection to be driven by teacher candidate content and context. However, it is questionable if the use of technology in this course has the "potential to transform education not because of the affordances of any particular tool but because it creates a new ecology of learning that fosters collaboration, communication, and creativity" (Mirra, 2018, p. 1). This conundrum for English teacher educators reoccurs regularly across all aspects of the study. It is clear that technology supports the learning of the conceptual, procedural, and attitudinal knowledge specific to the teaching of the English language arts and it is a tool that supports teacher candidates' instructional practices, but the question remains if this usage moves past the level of active engagement to creating new content, new knowledge, and new tasks (Hsieh, 2018; Mirra, 2018; Rowsell et al., 2017).

Across the study, the 8% of the syllabi that exemplified active engagement with technology (see Table 2.4) were analyzed to provide a portrait of which methods, applications, and multiple literacies were being engaged in the methods class such as the previous case illustrates. Analysis looked to trace the changes in concept and practice taking place across all syllabi deemed engaging technology at an active level, the 3% for learning the content of teaching English and the 5% for teaching how to learn English. Two of the syllabi were courses taught completely online, with another as a hybrid, and all others delivered in traditional in-person classrooms. These nine methods courses were emblematic of the overall findings from the study regarding active engagement with sustained technology integration. However, each case is a portrait of an English language arts methods class in time, providing a snapshot of a program grappling with the tensions and rewards of incorporating technology into the teaching and learning of English. Thus, some English teacher education programs have moved past the tensions described in Chapters 3 and 4, while others are just beginning to experience similar issues today.

The most commonly used open and closed technologies in the classes that actively engaged students with technology included course management systems for work submission, video for reflective practice purposes, internet assignments for locating and evaluating professional resources, rhetorical analysis of websites, multimodal composition, and online discussion or journaling. These recurring methods and technologies will be discussed in more detail in Chapter 3 in relation to how each course actively engaged students with technology in their methods classes for *learning* to teach English.

Notes

1. This chapter draws on research data and discussions previously published as manuscripts, Pasternak, D.L., Hallman, H.L., Caughlan, S., Renzi, L., Rush, L.S., & Meineke, H. (2016). Learning and teaching technology in English teacher

education: Findings from a national study. *Contemporary Issues in Technology and Teacher Education.* 16(1). Pasternak, D.L., Caughlan, Hallman, H.L., S., Renzi, & L., Rush, L.S. (2018). *Secondary English Teacher Education in the United States.* London, UK: Bloomsbury Academic supported by the University of Wisconsin Milwaukee (UWM) School of Education, the UWM Graduate School, and the UWM Research Growth Initiative.

2. For a detailed description of the overall study and its respondents, see Pasternak et al. (2018) Appendix A: Research Study Design: A Mixed-Methods Study of English Teacher Education, pp. 177–186.

3. There were 22 focus group participants from a range of geographical locations, program sizes, and English and education departments across the US. See Pasternak et al. (2018) for a breakdown of institution type and number of completers.

References

Blair, J., Czaja, R., & Blair, E. (2014). *Designing surveys: A guide to decisions and procedures.* Los Angeles, CA: Sage.

Council for the Accreditation of Educator Preparation (CAEP). (2015). *The Standards.* Retrieved from http://caepnet.org/standards/introduction

edTPA. (2019). *Home.* Retrieved from www.edtpa.com/

Ertmer, P. A. (2005). Teacher pedagogical beliefs: The final frontier in our quest for technology integration? *Educational Technology Research and Development,* 53(4), 25–39.

Foulger, T. S., Graziano, K. J., Schmidt-Crawford, D., & Slykhuis, D. A. (2017). Teacher educator technology competencies. *Journal of Technology and Teacher Education,* 25(4), 413–448.

George, M., Pope, C., & Reid, L. (2015). Contemporary literacies and technologies in English language arts teacher education: Shift happens! *Contemporary Issues in Technology and Teacher Education,* 15(1), 1–13. Retrieved from www.citejournal.org/vol15/iss1/languagearts/article1.cfm

Gorder, L. M. (2008). A study of teacher perceptions of instructional technology integration in the classroom. *Delta Pi Epsilon Journal,* 50(2), 63–76.

Guzman, A., & Nussbaum, M. (2009). Teaching competencies for technology integration in the classroom. *Journal of Computer Assisted Learning,* 25(5), 453–469.

Harris, J., Mishra, P., & Koehler, M. (2009). Teachers' technological pedagogical content knowledge and learning activity types: Curriculum-based technology integration reframed. *Journal of Research on Technology in Education (International Society for Technology in Education),* 41(4), 393–416.

Hsieh, B. (2018). This is how we do it: Authentic and strategic technology use by novice English teachers. *Contemporary Issues in Technology and Teacher Education,* 18(2), 271–288.

International Society for Technology in Education (ISTE). (2019). *Standards.* Retrieved from www.iste.org/standards

Mirra, N. (2018, July 3). Connected learning and 21st century English teacher education [Blog post]. *Educator Innovator.* Retrieved from https://educatorinnovator.org/connected-learning-and-21st-century-english-teacher-education

National Council for Accreditation of Teacher Education (NCATE). (1997). *Technology and the New Professional Teacher: Preparing for the 21st Century Classroom*. Retrieved from https://eric.ed.gov/?id=ED412201

National Council of Teachers of English (NCTE). (2013). The NCTE definition of 21st century literacies. *NCTE Position Statements*. Retrieved from www2.ncte.org/statement/21stcentdefinition/

National Council of Teachers of English (NCTE). (2018). Beliefs for integrating technology into the English language arts classroom. *NCTE Position Statements*. Retrieved from www2.ncte.org/statement/beliefs-technology-preparation-english-teachers/

National Council for the Teachers of English (NCTE),National Council for Accreditation of Teacher Education (NCATE). (2012). *NCTE/NCATE Standards for the Initial Preparation of Teachers of Secondary English Language Arts, Grades 7–12*. Retrieved from www.google.com/url?sa=t&rct=j&q=&esrc=s&source=web&cd=4&ved=2ahUKEwje58H3tJLkAhUPIKwKHfeIBYkQFjADegQIBBAC&url=http%3A%2F%2Fwww.ncte.org%2Flibrary%2FNCTEFiles%2FGroups%2FCEE%2FNCATE%2FApprovedStandards_111212.pdf&usg=AOvVaw2D4d86eick89uqH4SQEbqk

Nelson, M. J., Voithofer, R., & Cheng, S. (2019). Mediating factors that influence the technology integration practices of teacher educators. *Computers & Education*, *128*, 330–344.

Ottenbreit-Leftwich, A. T., Ertmer, P. A., & Tondeur, J. (2015). Interpretation of research on technology integration in teacher education in the USA: Preparation and current practices. In P. Smeyers, D. Bridges, N. C. Burbules, & M. Griffiths (Eds.), *International handbook of interpretation in educational research* (pp. 1239–1262). New York, NY: Springer.

Pasternak, D. L. (2007). Is technology used as practice? A survey analysis of preservice English teachers' perceptions and classroom practices. *Contemporary Issues in Technology and Teacher Education* [Online serial], *7*(3), 140–157. Retrieved from www.citejournal.org/volume-7/issue-3-07/english-language-arts/is-technology-used-as-practice-a-survey-analysis-of-pre-service-english-teachers-perceptions-and-classroom-practices

Pasternak, D. L., Caughlan, S., Hallman, H., Renzi, L., & Rush, L. (2018). *Secondary English teacher education in the United States*. Reinventing Teacher Education Series. London, UK: Bloomsbury Academic.

Pasternak, D. L., Hallman, H. L., Caughlan, S., Renzi, L., Rush, L. S., & Meineke, H. (2016). Learning and teaching technology in English teacher education: Findings from a national study. *Contemporary Issues in Technology & Teacher Education*, *16*(1), 373–387. Retrieved from www.citejournal.org/volume-16/issue-4-16/english-language-arts/learning-and-teaching-technology-in-english-teacher-education-findings-from-a-national-study

Pierson, M. E. (2001). Technology integration practice as a function of pedagogical expertise. *Journal of Research on Computing in Education*, *33*(4), 413.

Rowsell, J., Morrell, E., & Alvermann, D. E. (2017). Confronting the digital divide: Debunking brave new world discourses. *The Reading Teacher*, *71*(2), 157–165. doi:10.1002/trtr.1603

Rust, J., & Cantwell, D. (2018). No one fits in a box: Preservice teachers' evolving perceptions of self and others. *Contemporary Issues in Technology and Teacher Education*, *18*(2), 313–342. Retrieved from www.citejournal.org/volume-18/issue-2-18/english-language-arts/no-one-fits-in-a-box-preservice-teachers-evolving-perceptions-of-self-and-others

Shelton, C. (2018). "You have to teach to your personality": Caring, sharing and teaching with technology. *Australasian Journal of Educational Technology*, *34*(4), 92–106.

Thieman, G. Y. (2008). Using technology as a tool for learning and developing 21st century citizenship skills: An examination of the NETS and technology use by preservice teachers with their K-12 students. *Contemporary Issues in Technology and Teacher Education*, *8*(4), 342–366. Retrieved from www.citejournal.org/volume-8/issue-4-08/social-studies/using-technology-as-a-tool-for-learning-and-developing-21st-century-citizenship-skills-an-examination-of-the-nets-and-technology-use-by-pre-service-teachers-with-their-k-12-students/

United States Department of Education, Office of Educational Technology. (2017). *National Education Technology Plan*. Retrieved from https://tech.ed.gov

3 Integrating Technology to Learn English Language Arts Methods

This chapter investigates the integration of technology in the methods course that focuses on how teacher educators ask their teacher candidates to employ technology to learn course content. As discussed in Chapter 2, university students use technology to apply and enroll at a university, register for classes, contact faculty and staff, and engage in their learning communities inside and outside of in-person and virtual classroom spaces. Most take online tests through course management systems and read digital texts in various modes and forums. Teacher candidates will ultimately be assessed on their fitness to teach through e-portfolios, like the edTPA (2019) or other assessment systems of this ilk, which incorporate word processing and video. Hence, technology is a major part of the university experience, and many educators view their students as digital natives who are not in need of direct instruction regarding technology integration. This belief was evident throughout the syllabi analysis.

Certain types of technology were mentioned frequently by the teacher educators who completed the open answer responses in the questionnaire, submitted syllabi, and participated in the focus group discussions as standard practices in support of their teacher candidates to learn the methods of teaching English. These technologies fell into two groupings that are not mutually exclusive (see Chapter 1): (1) technology that *opens* spaces for collaborative learning, such as wikis, blogs, discussion boards, and online tutoring; and (2) discrete technologies that act as utilitarian or supplemental tools that *close* spaces to support individualized learning or assess that learning.

When asked in the questionnaire "how do methods courses address using digital technology in teaching and learning" (see Table 3.1), respondents indicated that both collaborative (open technologies) and discrete technologies (closed technologies) were used by teacher candidates to learn the content of the methods course, while somewhat fewer in each category had them design lessons using technology to teach English language arts content.

Table 3.1 How Do Methods Courses Address Using Digital Technologies in Teaching and Learning?

Open *technologies (e.g., wikis, blogs, online tutoring): n = 177*			
To Learn	Design Lessons for Course	Design Lessons for Field	Median Options Chosen
74.0	63.5	43.5	2

Closed *technologies (e.g., portfolios, multimodal software): n = 177*			
To Learn	Design Lessons for Course	Design Lessons for Field	Median Options Chosen
75.1	67.1	49.7	2

Note: Values as percent of respondents who chose each option (check all that apply).

However, the respondents indicated that once their teacher candidates were in their clinicals, there was a significant drop in the expectation that their lessons would address some type of technology integration into their own teaching and learning. As indicated in Table 3.1, technology is primarily integrated into the methods course more frequently for learning the content of the methods course than as English language arts content. There may be a number of different factors that affect the decrease in how technology is employed for teaching and learning across English teacher education programs, which may include philosophical, generational, or social reasons (see Chapter 2). However, when looked at across learning experiences, technology integration is generally used in the methods class to learn content more so than integrated into a teacher candidate's instructional practices, with a significant drop in expectation of usage in the clinical experience (see Table 3.1). In analyzing the syllabi collected for the study, the differences between integrating technology for learning and for teaching show similar results to the questionnaire's findings (compare Table 3.1 and see Table 2.4).

Learning, Which Technology?

Only one syllabus of the 136 collected for the study demonstrated that technology was engaged actively by teacher candidates for *both* learning the content of the methods course and integrating it into their own teaching practices (see Chapter 2). This syllabus did underscore that technology supported the learning of conceptual, procedural, and attitudinal knowledge specific to the teaching of the English language arts. It was a tool for learning that supported instructional practices in the English language arts.

However, it was unclear how the usage of technology demonstrated in any of the syllabi collected for this study actively engaged teacher candidates and moved them to act independently to create new knowledge and new tasks—a further indication of the continued unevenness in the integrate of technology in the teaching and learning of English.

One syllabus demonstrated that technology was integrated for *both* teaching and learning. Therefore, the remainder of the syllabi were divided into two groups, those that focused on technology (1) for learning the content of the methods course or (2) for teaching the content of English (see Chapter 4 for technology for teaching English). Technology for learning generally focused on technology that closed spaces for assessment or individual learning purposes. The most commonly used technologies for learning methods content included submitting work and reading course materials through a course management system, videotaping for reflective practice purposes, rhetorically analyzing internet websites for locating and evaluating professional resources, creating multimodal research papers with one technology component, and journaling or participating in online discussion forums about methods course materials. However, teacher candidates were often asked to engage with open technology to discuss course materials with their peers through wikis, blogs, and discussion boards—in some cases, even email.

Across the syllabi submitted for analysis, teacher candidates were variously required to use technology specifically to navigate the course's infrastructure and submit course materials through a course management system, such as Blackboard, Canvas, or Desire2Learn; download resources from websites; communicate with instructors and peers via email or social media; blog, journal, or reflect with classmates about their required reading or experiences teaching by engaging with each other through online discussion boards or wikis; maintain online portfolios; or submit licensure documents online. Many of the teacher educators required some type of readings about technology and multiple literacies (see Table 2.4) in their methods courses. Some required only a single activity or approach to be explored one time or through minor active engagement with it. To supplement the assigned readings or discussion of technology, teacher candidates were sometimes required to address technology at least once in their planning, instruction, or presentation of content. Methods course instructors asked their teacher candidates to repeat one activity, such as submit materials in a course management system, create a blog as an isolated assignment, or have an email discussion. Rubrics were mostly taught through online applications and PowerPoint was the named technology as the presentation platform.

Three syllabi demonstrated sustained or active engagement with technology integration for learning. Those syllabi were back-traced to the study participant's responses to the fixed and open-ended question portions of the questionnaire and forward-traced to the focus group discussions to provide additional insight or clarification to requirements indicated in the syllabus. None of the focus group participants submitted a syllabus that was analyzed as actively engaging technology integration for learning. It should be unsurprising that the methods courses that heavily integrated technology for learning were conducted through hybrid or online delivery. What follows is a critical discussion of those classes as snapshots in time of how programs unevenly grapple with the integration of technology to learn methods content. If possible, each course was put into the context of its program structure. The chapter ends with a discussion of replicating in-person courses online.

Reflection and Inquiry: Technology as a Tool for Learning

Reflection and Inquiry in Secondary English Teaching Practices I is the first methods course in a series of methods classes, all offered in a hybrid format. The teacher candidates enrolled in the class met in person seven times with asynchronous online meetings taking place during the rest of the semester. Taken concurrently with a full-year clinical experience over the first semester of the "intern"[1] year, participants were asked to work "through various modules on the wiki, posting and responding to videos on Viddler [a cost-based interactive online video platform] and writing reflections based on given topics." The instructor's welcome statement indicates,

> We will investigate a) how to move toward dialogic approaches to instruction, b) how to use video and other technologies to conduct inquiries about our teaching, and c) how to open our practice through video work and sustained conversations with field instructors, mentor teachers, and peers in order to improve student learning.

Offered through a school or department of education, this general English methods class focused on using technology to reflect upon learning how to teach English; aligned standards and objectives to this focus by using closed technology to assess compliance; and employed open technologies to create collaborative experiences between teacher candidates in the field, experienced English teachers, field instructors, and each other through online discussion. Virtual professional learning communities were formed by grouping peers in similar contexts, video response groups, inquiry groups, and/or grade level groups.

In using technology, the English teacher educator challenged the course participants as to how they might "observe and reflect on [y]our own practice (through videotaping, reflection, collaboration, and other means), so that you continue to grow." There is an online journal requirement that used open technology to engage teacher candidates in discussion about "big issue topics;" however as a closed technology space, the educator used it to assess teacher knowledge and engagement with the discussion topics. Work was submitted through a course management system where the teacher candidates could find additional readings, videos, and other resources through the class wiki. However, none of the print texts required for purchase listed on the syllabus covered any technology or new literacy content. It is worth noting the one technology policy regarding the purchase of a "memory card" to ensure data retention, because:

> Over the course of the year, we will be doing extensive work with video, video editing and online, video-based social networking. To facilitate this work, we are asking that you purchase one memory card for use in 1) the camera, and 2) the laptop. Please store ALL of your video for the entire semester on this card. We are recommending the SanDisk Ultra II, 4GB with USB port for easy use across technologies.

This policy seems apropos, because the bulk of the coursework was reserved for creating and reflecting on the creation of two video postings in Viddler,

> **Video Post 1, 20%:** This project will involve 1) video-taping a full period of teaching, 2) selecting and posting a 5–10-minute video clip that offers evidence of student learning, 3) responding to the videos of a small group of colleagues, 4) assessing your instruction, 5) assessing student responses to instruction, and 6) generating revisions, refinements, and ideas for future plans.
> **Video Post 2, 20%:** This project will again involve video-taping your teaching and selecting and posting a 5–10-minute video clip. However, for this video post, you are invited to document some aspect of your practice that you would like to study for your inquiry project. Again, you will respond to the videos of your small group, but this time, you will use a specific inquiry strategy to systematically assess some aspect of your teaching.

The teacher educator who submitted this syllabus explained in the open-ended response portion of the questionnaire that "Our students also video-tape themselves teaching, post clips to online, small-group discussion sites, and respond to each others' teaching several times during the intern year." When asked what types of open or closed technology were required in your program, this respondent indicated "To prepare a portfolio for end-of-program evaluation."

However, despite the extensive use of technology to learn to teach English that is evidenced through Reflection and Inquiry in Secondary English Teaching Practices I, it is worth noting that the teacher candidates in this program had the option of creating their portfolio for the end-of-program evaluation either through digital or paper submission. Artifacts that were selected for the "binder" included lesson and unit plans, reflections about their own teaching and from their teaching conferences that span the semester, observations notes, midterm and end-term evaluations, professional development plans, and other teaching records. Teacher candidates are instructed, "You do not need to bring this binder to our classes until we meet for the final exam, but your field instructor might be checking it regularly. You may feel free to create an electronic [binder] if that suits you. Your [binder] will be a great resource for you next year, as it will represent a year's worth of lesson plans for a single class."

Since many artifacts are indeed digital, why wouldn't the program expect *all* the artifacts to be kept and submitted digitally? Allowing the option for an electronic or a paper portfolio here speaks to the dilemma teacher education programs are faced with when requiring teacher candidates to have or use technology. Will the field supervisor have technology for evaluations, or will this person be limited to pen and paper observation instruments? If technology is available, will reports created through it be convenient to the teacher candidate, mentor, and field supervisor for referencing, reading, or feedback purposes? Lastly, if teacher candidates are required to videotape their classrooms and retain that data on a required SD card, do they have permission to videotape their students, and do all districts follow the same privacy rules? These are some of the challenges faced by teacher education programs even when they are invested in technology for learning course content such as in Reflection and Inquiry in Secondary English Teaching Practices I.

Web-Based Methods Classes: Closing and Opening Spaces for Learning

Teaching Literature within the Curriculum (Teaching Literature) is the first methods course in a two-methods course sequence. It is followed by Teaching Language Arts and Composition in the Middle School and Secondary School in Grades 5–12: Seminar and Field Experience (Teaching Language Arts). Both courses are housed in a department or school of education and delivered completely online. Each class requires one textbook with supplemental readings posted in the course management system, Blackboard. There are links to a website and a video to ensure adherence to APA style documentation as well as to a list of eight websites at the end of the syllabus that link to resources like Blooms Taxonomy, *Rubistar*, state standards, etc., all of which are indicated through their URLs without website titles (a frequent occurrence across all the syllabi). Teaching Literature's required print text includes one chapter concerning reading texts in "other formats," which is a discussion of comics and other graphic formats in young adult literature. There is little mention of digital texts in this chapter. The second course in the sequence, Teaching Language Arts, has one chapter on new literacies in the required printed text.

The first methods class, Teaching Literature, specifies one course objective that addresses technology integration that aligns with a number of assignments, indicating that "Preservice and graduate level language arts teachers and librarians will be able to design lessons and units for diverse learners using differentiated instruction, making use of effective research based practices, including the appropriate use of technology." Teacher candidates engage a number of open and closed technologies. Requirements include participation in an online community at *Teaching Literature to Adolescents* (2016) through a link in the syllabus to discuss teaching the novel *Holes* with other teachers and teacher candidates. Additionally, the teacher candidates participate in a web quest as well as role-play one of the *Holes* characters by blogging with their peers about the book. Apart from the character blog and participation in the *Teaching Literature to Adolescents* online community, the teacher candidates engage their classmates weekly in an online discussion forum in Blackboard. To conduct the weekly Blackboard discussions, there are links to digital resources concerning standards or teaching practices and assessments. There is a research paper requirement called the Content Knowledge assignment that details "when and how technology can be used and successfully integrated into the assignment and/or the subsequent differentiated instruction." A specific rubric assesses the overall, individual requirements under consideration in this assignment with a section that evaluates the teacher candidate's technology knowledge in the excerpt that follows (see Table 3.2).

It is worth noting that technology integration is only one aspect of this assignment, with other sections that include analyzing middle and high school student work and learning, plus identifying strategies to improve student achievement. Other technologies employed include the requirement to use *Rubistar* (2008) to design assessments included in the teacher candidates' five-day plans after reading about rubrics. There is a link to the digital article and to the website in the syllabus to learn this content.

Like those already explained above, rubrics were provided for almost all coursework submissions in the syllabi. Specifically, the Blackboard discussion forum rubric was quite detailed, which may be understandable as it is the major forum for teacher candidate engagement with materials and peers (see Table 3.3).

Table 3.2 Sample Rubric 1: Technology Integration (from Teaching Literature within the Curriculum)

CATEGORY	Exceeds Expectations 4	Meets Expectations 2	Below Expectations 1
Technology	The candidate demonstrated the ability to justify when and how to successfully integrate instructional technologies into his/her assessment and/or subsequent differentiated instruction.	The candidate demonstrated the ability to integrate instructional technologies into his/her assessment and/or subsequent differentiated instruction.	The candidate did not properly use instructional technologies in his/her assessment and/or subsequent differentiated instruction and/or could not justify why the use of technology was not appropriate.

Table 3.3 Sample Rubric 2: Blackboard Discussion Posting (from Teaching Literature within the Curriculum)

Your Grade for the *Discussion Board* Postings for Each Discussion Session Will Be Based on the Following Criteria

27–30 Points [Bolding in Original]

- Discussion contributions are responsive to the requirement of the Discussion instruction requirements and are posted on time.
- Discussion contributions significantly enhance the quality of interaction (e.g. illustrate a point with examples, suggest new perspectives on an issue, ask thought-provoking questions), provide constructive feedback to colleagues, and raise opposing viewpoint in a polite manner.
- Discussion contributions demonstrate an in-depth understanding of concept and issues presented in the course. And contain insightful interpretations of, or well-supported alternative viewpoints on, the content as applicable.
- Discussion contributions provide evidence that the student has read and considered a sampling of colleagues' postings and synthesized key comments and ideas, as applicable.

24–26 Points

- Discussion contributions are responsive to the requirement of the Discussion instruction requirements and are posted on time.
- Discussion contributions contribute to the quality of interaction (e.g. illustrate a point with examples, suggest new perspectives on an issue, ask thought-provoking questions), provide constructive feedback to colleagues, and raise opposing viewpoint in a polite manner.
- Discussion contributions demonstrate a minimal understanding of concept and issues presented in the course and are generally accurate but contain some omissions and/or errors.

(Continued)

Table 3.3 (Continued)

- Discussion contributions do not provide evidence that the student has read and considered a least some colleagues' postings or synthesized key comments and ideas, as applicable.

1–23 Points

- Discussion contributions are posted by the due date but are not always responsive to the requirements of the Discussion instructions.
- Discussion contributions do little to enhance the quality of interaction and rarely include questions or comments that stimulate thinking and learning.
- Discussion contributions demonstrate a minimal understanding of concept and issues presented in the course and are generally accurate but contain some omissions and/or errors.
- Discussion contributions do not provide evidence that the student has read and considered a least some colleagues' postings or synthesized key comments and ideas, as applicable.

0 Points

- Discussion contributions are posted past the late deadline, defined as 11:59, PT on the last day of the week in which the assignment is due, and /or do not address the requirements of the Discussion instructions.
- Discussion contributions do little do not contribute to the quality of interaction and do not include questions or comments that stimulate thinking and learning.
- Discussion contributions do not demonstrate an understanding of concept and issues presented in the course. and/or contain omissions and/or errors.
- Discussion contributions do not provide evidence that the student has read or considered colleagues' postings as applicable.

The discussion forum rubric (see Table 3.3) is similar to the one created for the Weekly Chapter Review Discussion Board, although that one centers on demonstrating "an in-depth understanding, appropriate use, and correct implementation of the theories, concepts, and/or strategies presented in the course materials" found in the weekly assigned readings, in alignment with the assignment components and adherence to academic writing standards. Graduate students have a specific, named technology assignment in that they were required to create a PowerPoint to demonstrate their knowledge of "current trends on integrating literature in the curriculum." The professor seems to be the sole audience for this assignment, and its submission must adhere to strict guidelines:

> At least six slides in your presentation, font used on the slides should be easy to read, include at least one animation, one use of clip art or pictures, one use of audio and video, and one use of an internet hot link, or u tube [sic] video.

Its rubric follows.

***Scoring Guide for Graduate PowerPoint Presentation* [Bolding in Original]**

Included at least six slides in presentation	20 points.
Font used in presentation easy to read	20 points.
Included at least one use of animation	15 points.
Includes at least one use of clip art or pictures	15 points.
Included at least one use of audio and video	15 points.
Included at least one use of an internet hot link	15 points.
Content answered the prompt	25 points.

It seems that all the assignments indicated in the first class, Teaching Literature, except for the weekly discussion forums, were to be completed early in the semester and submitted through Blackboard. As to technology policies, there is a strict attendance policy which explains what virtual attendance involves:

> Students participating in an online course at [name of university] are required to log in to each of their online courses and participate on a weekly basis. Likewise, all [name of university] faculty are required to check students [sic] attendance/participation on a weekly basis and report attendance through the [name of university] Faculty Portal System. All online faculty check attendance as "present" if the students have logged in one or more times during that week. Saturday is the day on which attendance is checked and submitted to [name of university]. Students that have NOT logged in during a given week PRIOR to Saturday will be counted as absent for that week. Absences will affect grades.

The attendance policy parallels the university's academic dishonesty policy, which addresses the submission of digital coursework, notifying students that all coursework will be checked through Blackboard's product *SafeAssign* (2019). The use of this technology is worthy of note considering it possibly only affects students learning in a virtual environment. However, it is possible that even students enrolled in in-person classes may be required to submit assignments through the Blackboard portal:

> By submitting assignments, you agree to have SafeAssign software check the originality and intellectual integrity of your work. You acknowledge and understand that upon submission, your paper will

be added to the [name of university] database and compared against a global database of submitted papers. You further recognize that the determination of academic dishonesty rests with the instructor of this course and that plagiarism will be dealt with according to the policy set forth in the [name of university] Student Handbook.

This technology policy requires students to submit their work for scrutiny to stem academic dishonesty. It is the only one of this ilk that I found throughout all the syllabi submitted for the study. *SafeAssign* may be used for in-person classes as well as online courses, but the only time this software is mentioned in any of the syllabi is for this online class. Therefore, the unstated presumption that online learning may be more prone to attract students who cheat rather than those who take in-person classes, adds an additional layer of tension to integrate technology not seen elsewhere in the study. The implication that online learning environments may be more supportive of people who cheat at their education than those who view online learning as a convenience could create an atmosphere of distrust not necessarily found in in-person classrooms, and an impression of course delivery and the students who enroll in them that may affect how a teacher candidate views online learning.

The second semester course in this online sequence, Teaching Language Arts and Composition in the Middle School and Secondary School in Grades 5–12: Seminar and Field Experience, does not differ too widely in its design, rubrics, or expectations from Teaching Literature. Again, the teacher candidates regularly engage with each other reflectively about course content in a discussion forum or the class blog. The teacher candidates are assigned digital study readings and videos to watch from websites. Like Teaching Literature, there is one course objective that specifies technology integration. In this class, technology must be integrated into the five-day lesson:

> The student will be able to create 5-day lesson plans that demonstrates an obvious understanding of, sensitivity to and appreciation for diversity in all forms. The plans and activities will provide clear evidence of the students' ability to meet the needs of diverse learners by providing differentiated and culturally sensitive responses to learners' academic and social needs, making use of effective research based practices and including the appropriate use of technology.

The language "appropriate use of technology" is seen frequently throughout many of the syllabi collected for the study. However, it is worth noting that what constitutes appropriate usage does not seem to be defined for the teacher candidates when this language is included in the objectives or elsewhere in the syllabus. Perhaps what constitutes appropriate technology usage will be lectured upon or assigned as a research project in this sequence's Content Knowledge assignment, which, like in Teaching Literature syllabus, teacher candidates are required to "explain when and how technology can be used and successfully integrated into the assignment and/or the subsequent differentiated instruction." Technology is a specific topic in the discussion forum once. Teacher candidates must discuss "How can we use Twitter and Blogs in the LA [language arts] classroom?" Perhaps what is considered appropriateness in technology usage will emerge through this discussion.

Graduate students have an additional assignment that addresses technology, like in the Teaching Literature syllabus. They must create a group wiki on differentiation in the classroom. However, each graduate student composes her or his own page of the wiki, so it is unclear how this experience is collaborative, or if the wiki is public or has any audience other than the instructor.

As all the teacher candidates in this class are in concurrent clinical placements and will be assessed on the integration of technology in their five-day plans, it would be remiss not to consider that there are no other stated requirements that technology be engaged in the clinical placement. However, the requirement to develop technology integration in the five-day plan is unclear as to if those plans will be taught during the clinical or if there is a supplemental course syllabus for the clinical placements that spells out technology requirements in the field.

As is evident from both these courses, open and closed technology is used for learning the content of the methods course—sometimes with implementation not mutually exclusive to the type of integration. For instance, the discussion forum in Blackboard and from the *Teaching Adolescent Literature* website opens the teacher candidates up to collaboration with their peers. However, those forums are still used to assess participant engagement and follow strict guidelines regarding the number, breadth, and depth of postings. The character blog seems like a way to assess understanding of characterization or if, in fact, the novel was read for closed assessment purposes. What is more though, taking on a digital persona may be a learning experience to collaborate with peers through role-playing that may allow for the participant to create new knowledge and new tasks (Hsieh, 2018; Mirra, 2018; Rowsell, Morrell, & Alvermann, 2017). In remaining anonymous, an experience not afforded to people engaging in in-person role-playing, there are opportunities that differ from in-person role-playing.

Substituting Technology for In-Person Classrooms

When integrating technology into the English language arts for learning, teacher educators ask their students to learn with technology slightly more often than they ask them to integrate it into their teaching practices. Once teacher candidates enter their clinical experiences, they are required even less so to integrate it (see Table 3.1) into their learning. The reasons for the decrease in integration span tensions around access to technology as well as philosophical, generational, or social preferences in teaching styles and knowledge.

The technologies most prevalently integrated into teacher candidate learning included both open technology, predominantly to collaborate with peers, and closed technologies, mostly for assessment of content knowledge purposes, which included navigating a course management system to read course materials, submit assignments, engage in online discussion or journaling, and reflect on the success of a teaching segment videotaped for that purpose.

It could be argued that the technology required in all three of the classes detailed in this chapter do not reach the level of critical usage or inquiry most teacher educators would want from their own teacher candidates (see Chapter 2). Few of the requirements described here allow for the creation of new knowledge or support conceptual, procedural, or attitudinal knowledge. Despite active engagement with technology throughout the courses to support the learning of English language arts methods to online students, technology here is mostly a utilitarian tool that allows for teacher candidates to come together in a virtual forum that merely substitutes for an in-person classroom for expediency purposes. When the teacher candidates are required to integrate technology into their own teaching, across all three classes, they are asked to integrate it into their teaching once in their planning, instruction, or presentation of content, often not mirroring the technologies they are already using for their own education. Of course, this disparity might be indicative of the clinical placement not having similar technology or there being a range of clinical placements that have technology of varying types and degrees.

There is tension between requiring teacher candidates to submit digital or paper portfolios for end-of-program evaluation. This situation may be a result of inconsistent access or instructor preferences. Moreover, technology becomes overseer when used as a tool to ensure academic honesty and the integrity of the higher education classroom.

Despite how all three classes have teacher candidates actively engage technology in a sustained manner throughout the semester, none did so on a *critical* level (see Chapter 2). Although the rubrics from the online course sequence were detailed, it is unclear if the technologies engaged in were taught with explicit instruction or merely assigned as an expected skill in an online or hybrid class.

This question about explicit instruction arose in the focus group discussion. In discussing his own program, focus group participant Charles Bates (see Chapter 2) explained that in his program, technology integration was mostly Prezi or PowerPoint presentation, integration somewhat like the courses focused on in this chapter. Other focus group participants Anita Vogel and Caroline Stewart mentioned that technology needs to be integrated not for "the sake of technology," but seamlessly around the purpose of the technology. Stewart exemplified her remarks by explaining how Skype could be used to invite experts into a classroom. Other methods instructors felt that studying multimodal texts generated rich discussions about technology usage among teacher candidates—technologies that require time, thought, and practice for both the teacher educators and candidates, which may not be available in a semester-long methods class where the teacher educator needs to cover all the other content an English teacher must learn how to teach. This topic, integrating technology into one's own teaching practices, will be discussed in detail in Chapter 4 in relation to how each of the classes highlighted engaged teacher candidates with both open and closed technologies in their methods classes for the *teaching* of English.

Note

1. The terms intern and internship in this syllabus seems analogous to what most English teacher educators call a field student and/or student teacher experiencing a traditional field and student teaching placement.

References

Beach, R., Appleman, D., Fecho, B., & Simon, R. (2016). *Teaching Literature to Adolescents, 3rd Edition Companion Website*. Retrieved from http://teachingliterature. pbworks.com/w/page/19920355/FrontPage

edTPA. (2019). *Home*. Retrieved from www.edtpa.com/

Hsieh, B. (2018). This is how we do it: Authentic and strategic technology use by novice English teachers. *Contemporary Issues in Technology and Teacher Education*, 18(2). 271–288.

Mirra, N. (2018, July 03). Connected learning and 21st century English teacher education [Blog post]. *Educator Innovator*. Retrieved from https://educatorinnovator. org/connected-learning-and-21st-century-english-teacher-education

Rowsell, J., Morrell, E., & Alverman, D.E. (2017). Confronting the digital divide: Debunking brave new world discourses. *The Reading Teacher*, 71(2). 157–165. doi:10.1002/trtr.1603

Rubistar (2008). Home. Retrieved from http://rubistar.4teachers.org/index.php

SafeAssign (2019). Retrieved from https://www.blackboard.com/teaching-learning/ learning-management/safe-assign

4 Integrating Technology to Teach English

In this chapter, I discuss which technologies teacher educators require their teacher candidates to integrate into their own teaching practices. Throughout the various phases of the study, teacher educators named specific technologies they thought important for their teacher candidates to know and employ in their own teaching practices and lessons. Sometimes these practices were modeled in the course content and/or in the course requirements. When the course focused on technology for teaching, teacher candidates were required to incorporate technology into their own lessons to meet whichever standards the teacher educator followed. Such as, teacher candidates were expected to employ a course management system in a lesson, teach a lesson on multiple or new literacies, create a blog (wiki, discussion forum) for middle and secondary grade school students to engage with each other collaboratively, teach the purpose of technology, engage in digital storytelling, have students electronically communicate through social media or email, design a grade book or assessment rubric, present materials through interactive whiteboards or presentation applications, analyze the use of technology in a lesson, or tutor online. However, many times, the type of technology was left unspecified for integration and often just labeled *technology* in the requirement despite the sustained, engaged use expected of the teacher candidates. Technologies that were named spanned *opened* spaces for collaboration but also *closed* spaces for individualized, accountability purposes.

Like the syllabi analyzed in Chapter 3 for integrating technology for learning how to teach English, the syllabi in this chapter were selected for discussion because they indicated that teacher candidates were explicitly required to demonstrate sustained use of technology following the four-point coding scale (see Table 2.3). I used this scale to evaluate the level of engagement teacher candidates would have with technology in their methods class for all 136 syllabi. The results were similar between syllabi that indicated technology integration for learning and the ones that indicated technology for teaching (see Table 2.4), in that most technology integration was taught at the *awareness* or passive engagement level, meaning that technology was either mentioned in the course's standards and objectives or through assigned readings, but there was no indication in the assignments described in the syllabi that teacher candidates were required to integrate that technology into their teaching practices. Eighteen percent of the syllabi (see Table 2.4) described one specific assignment that involved technology that was not sustained throughout the course's other assignments or activities. Five percent of the syllabi, or six syllabi, did indicate sustained *active* engagement with technology integration with at least one or multiple assignments explicitly required. Those syllabi were then back-traced to the study participant's responses to the fixed and open-ended question portions of the questionnaire and forward-traced to the focus group discussions to provide additional insight or clarification to a practice(s). None of the focus group participants submitted a syllabus that was analyzed as actively engaging technology integration for teaching.

The six syllabi detailed in this chapter were analyzed as methods courses that required teacher candidates to integrate technology into their own lessons through sustained, repeated engagement throughout the semester. The critical discussion that follows explores the requirements, assignments, activities, and technologies required to teach English. Each class is a snapshot in time of how particular methods classes unevenly grappled with the integration of technology to teach English. The chapter ends with a discussion of that unevenness.

Optional, Learning to Teach English Online

Teaching English Inclusively is an in-person general English methods course offered through a school of education that emphasizes "secondary content and the [US state] ELA technological applications that apply to teaching and learning," focusing technology integration on state standards. Per this instructor's response in the open-ended questionnaire section of the study, teacher candidates select to learn how to "teach online courses" in this methods class. However, this content is not required of all people who take Teaching English Inclusively. To support teacher candidate success with the technology, additional technical and research support is provided for two specified hours each week by a university-based education librarian in addition to the class meeting times.

There are eight lesson plans required of the teacher candidates for 40% of the course grade, five of which require some specified type of technology integration. Each plan is submitted to both the instructor as well as all other class participants through a course management system. The plans adhere to guidelines for lesson planning set forth in Jim Burke's *English Teacher's Companion* and posted in the course management system. Burke's book is the one required print text and includes chapters on using technology and media literacy. The other required texts do not cover this content.

For the first lesson plan, the teacher candidates create and teach a lesson on rhetorically analyzing a website called "Teaching Us About the [fill in the blank] Web Site." The teacher candidates write up and submit their plans to their instructor and peers through the course management system prior to the 15 minutes allotted to them to engage their peers in the following steps:

- Taking us to your website;
- Highlighting what we can find;
- Doing an activity where we have to find something; and
- Sharing how you think this website might be useful, such as for working with the standards, the anticipatory set, our direct instruction, or a variety of assessments.

This assignment includes both open and closed technology for both teaching and learning, since they must construct a lesson that analyzes a website (teaching) and locate a professional resource (learning). However, there is a presumption in how the directions are stated that the teacher candidates can already navigate the web to find quality, professional resources. The teacher candidates learn website rhetorical analysis through finding a website (closed), then share their learning collaboratively with their peers (open). During this process, they are assessed on their knowledge of digital resources.

Their next two lessons, one on vocabulary and the other on grammar, must employ a video projector to present the highlights of the lessons to the teacher candidate's peers. With the fourth lesson, after reading the Burke chapter on technology usage, the teacher candidates create a lesson that focuses on some aspect of technology integration. This lesson is shared through the course management system and in-class using a video projector. This lesson must also include some type of unspecified assessment feature, but it is unclear if the assessment is technology-based. All these lessons use technology *tools* to deliver English language arts content, but it is unclear if that content is technology related.

Like the technology lesson, the fifth plan addresses media literacy with a focus on 21st century literacies created after the teacher candidates read about this content in the Burke text. The teacher candidates have the option of learning more about media literacy through resources in the course management system as well. Again, the plans are shared in class using a video projector. It is equally unclear what aspects of 21st century literacies and/or media literacy are the topics of these lessons and if they focus on technology. However, the content in the Burke chapter may dictate what these lessons entail.

The remainder of the required lesson plans and the unit plan do not have a direct, stated requirement to integrate technology in the content of the lesson. Moreover, it is uncertain what entails technology content except for the first lesson plan, when the teacher candidates are directed to create a lesson that rhetorically analyzes a website, and the fourth lesson plan, when they are directed to integrate technology. Are the teacher candidates required to use a website to design a rubric, analyze a page of the internet, employ digital storytelling, or create digital documents or forums? This part of the assignment is unclear.

Throughout the semester, all course work is shared through the course management system and through video presentation. There is an extensive list of websites included on the syllabus with no web page titles, just the URLs (a frequent occurrence across all the syllabi). It is unclear if the technology focused on in the early lesson plans build on the subsequent content and how those plans funnel into the unit plan.

Despite the assertion in the open-ended responses from the questionnaire portion of the study and the indication in the syllabus that people enrolled in Teaching English Inclusively may opt to learn how to teach English online, there are no specified lectures or readings in the course outline of events on that content. Like some of the courses detailed in Chapter 3 for learning English, it is worth noting that Teaching English Inclusively included a strict campus-based technology policy, similar to the one discussed in Chapter 2 that places restrictions on all wireless and electronic devices during class time and warned of technology's ability to cultivate academic dishonesty. As mentioned previously, technology policies such as this present a mixed, often confusing message to teacher candidates who are being required to integrate technology into their teaching and learning practices. On the one hand, these policies suggest that technology is disruptive, but on the other, teacher candidates are being required to find ways to bring it into their own teaching practices.

Technology Leading to the Teaching Practices Portfolio

Much technology integration leads to the compilation of a teaching portfolio. Secondary English Methods is an in-person one-credit general methods class with an additional emphasis "placed on the uses of technology." The course is housed in a school of education and its sole purpose is to create a portfolio of lessons that address technology integration. In the open-ended response portion of the questionnaire, its instructor stated that the "integration of technology is essential as another tool in research, reading and writing."

Secondary English Methods' learning objectives specify that "Candidates will identify and apply English methods, strategies and skills that reflect classroom best practices in the areas of [other areas, like management, critical thinking, etc.] and technology." The syllabus lists a specific technology objective or program goal in alignment with unit knowledge, skills, and dispositions. The teacher candidates are expected to "promote students' confidence in learning through the use of a variety of technological tools and a variety of learning materials and resources" by the teacher candidate using "technology appropriately and effectively for professional work."

Unlike many of the other methods course syllabi, this class has one of the *least* restrictive technology policies that were collected for the study. The teacher candidates in Secondary English methods are told,

> This course fosters the use of technology by providing opportunities and expectations for using the Internet, computer applications and [course management system] for discussion, research, and development of an E-folio for sharing documents.

This directive has the teacher candidates reflecting on each lesson they create through discussion board participation and developing an "e-folio." Assignments included in the e-folio include

1. "Create, document and annotate activities, lessons or presentations that align with" the lesson's objectives and NCTE standards. "At least two activities must include some form of technology, Ex. PowerPoint, Smart Board presentation, Virtual Field Trip, etc."
2. Compile an index/map of information/resources available on the NCTE website.
3. Select four of six suggested tasks, two of which integrate technology at some level into their practice:

    a. Compile and annotate a reference list of at least eight internet resource sites that you can use in your classroom instruction. These should include both instructional support and student research opportunities.
    b. Plan a fieldtrip [virtual or real world], which would enhance/accentuate instruction of an approved English topic.

Most of the technology required here closes spaces for assessment purposes, often substituting technology for more traditional library or presentation work. When asked to use technology for collaboration, it is used for reflection purposes by the teacher candidates to communicate with each other.

Building to a Technology Lesson Plan

Curriculum and Materials I is an in-person, general English methods course housed in a college of education. With an articulated focus on new and media literacy stated in the syllabus, the course requires Renee Hobbs' *Digital and Media Literacy: Connecting Culture and Classroom* and a recommendation to purchase texts that address the teaching of film. Despite this focus, neither the course goals nor objectives reference technology. However, the knowledge, skills, and dispositions indicated elsewhere in the syllabus specify alignment with the NCTE/IRA standards to "help students become media literate" using technology and informational and non-print resources. The syllabus includes the college's conceptual framework, illustrated in both a visual graphic and in print, indicating that technology is one of the six strands of knowledge that form the "basis for professional preparation" in the college.

For learning purposes, the course uses a course management system to house additional readings and links to videos, submit assignments, and conduct online discussion through a "message board." The online discussion focuses on responses to the course readings. However, these message board postings are expected to be accessible during class time and it is suggested that teacher candidates bring a print copy to class or have access to the discussion board through a phone, computer, or tablet. All materials must be processed using Microsoft Word.

For teaching purposes, teacher candidates produce a media production project and reflection that critically addresses "the classroom pros and cons" of media literacy on gender, ethnicity, lesson creation, and media production. Additionally, teacher candidates design, workshop, then submit a "revised media literacy lesson plan . . . that not only *uses* [italics in original] media but *teaches* [italics in original] about the media—access, analyze, evaluate or produce media messages." There are lectures and discussion postings on film techniques, media literacy, trends and tenets of media literacy, learning that is enhanced through media "but not as an end in itself," teaching with visuals and audio, and multiple literacies, all of which build to the creation and submission of the revised lesson plan that both uses and teaches media. This course actively builds to a media literacy lesson plan across the semester, asking students to engage technology in their teaching through reflection, theory, and practical applications.

Despite the sustained engagement with technology across the semester employing both open and closed technologies, as in many other syllabi, technology integration is expected but not explicitly named. As in Teaching English Inclusively, discussed earlier, it seems that it is up to the teacher candidate to come up with ideas or mirror what is suggested in the Hobbs' text (or Burke discussed earlier). With both classes, technology is being integrated into English lessons, but it is unclear if that means film, web-based or multimodal texts, or even just the use of voiceover Power-Point. However, even without the explicit details, this course seems to be one of the more successful examples of technology being integrated into the teaching of English.

Teaching With Technology But Not Learning With Technology

Teaching English is an in-person, general English methods class housed in a school of education. The syllabus presents a rationale from the instructor as to the aims of teaching, citing Laurillard's *Rethinking University Teaching: A Framework for the Effective Use of Educational Technology*. The course description indicates that the teacher candidates will study the "use of commercial and teacher-produced media." One of the required texts has a focus on new literacies and includes chapters on digital/media literacy in addition to "Internet and library research, audio/video resources" and links to a solid collection of internet professional resources for the teaching of English. Specific materials are required for the course, including a three-ring binder, a package of tab dividers, college-ruled notebook paper, blue and black pens, and a "SD card or Jump Drive with plenty of memory." Handwritten class notes and course resources are to be kept in an "organized form in the binder" for evaluation purposes.

One of the instructional objectives states that the teacher candidates will "Identify and use new technologies, multi-media applications, and other non-print resources that augment an effective English language arts program," and growth in being a "skilled, reflective and responsive teacher" will be measured through "reflections and response to performances through written critiques of personal, video-taped presentations" in collaboration with their peers.

Unit plans are presented to the class and video-recorded, with the plans demonstrating "visual aids using technology" and adhering to the following instructional guidelines:

A. Your primary visual aid will be PowerPoint. Use the unit subheadings and a few key words under each to help you remember what you want to say. You can also make up your own organizing device. The purpose is to help your audience follow your talk.

B. Other ideas to develop visuals—short lists of the following:

1. Identify Goals
2. Identify Student Actions (What will they do?)
3. Identify Assessment (What and how will you assess and measure learning and growth?)
4. Use related visuals, media, auditory aids, texts, etc. from the unit.

After their presentations, the teacher candidates have one week to critique their video presentations by adhering to the following:

A. Watch your video at least twice.
B. Write a 300–500-word essay discussing the strengths and weaknesses of your talk.
C. Consider the following:

1. How did you sound? Stand? Move? Did you seem comfortable with your technology?
2. Did the presentation include the key elements of your unit plan?
3. How did your explanations come across? If something was not clear, why?
4. How did the audience respond? How did you answer questions?
5. How did the actual performance compare to your plan of what it would be like?
6. After reflecting on your video, how will you change future presentations?

The course calendar indicates one class period devoted to a lecture on digital/media literacy, followed shortly by the first video presentation of the unit plan that integrates technology into teaching.

Considering the focus on technology in this class, there are policies that seem contradictory to its effective integration. Absent of a course management system, email cannot be used to submit assignments to the instructor; only paper submissions are accepted. There is a list of inappropriate classroom behaviors that dictate proper attire through technology usage which includes:

*   "The use of cellular phones is prohibited in class."
*   "The use of any type of audio device (such as an iPod) is prohibited in class. Likewise, earphones or headsets are prohibited in class."

- "If you are found using these devices in class (i.e., texting or listening to an audio device), you will be asked to leave the classroom, and you will receive an absence for the day."

These technology policies are highlighted by large, black arrows in the margins of the syllabus, communicating that the English studies classroom is not the appropriate place for technology usage, providing a contradictory environment for the teacher candidates required to integrate technology into their own practices but not use it in class. In this class, despite the creation of a unit plan focusing on "visual aids using technology," English seems like a subject separate from the technology, which seems to be a tool to merely deliver course content.

A Call for Content-Specific Technology Integration

The instructor for Pre-Professional Composition and Rhetoric, an in-person writing methods course housed in an English department, indicated in the open-ended response portion of the questionnaire that

> [T]he Methods courses should be central to addressing the integration of technology (i.e. TPAK). However, I do not feel that students have a strong foundation in the technology (from their 2 College of Ed instructional technology courses), and there are many other things to accomplish in methods, so I don't get to do quite as much as I wish.

This instructor's criticism of generic instructional technology courses points to the need for technology integration into the content specific methods classes. The teacher candidates in Pre-Professional Composition and Rhetoric have already taken two technology courses in their university's college of education; however, this English methods instructor sees a need for more content in this area, but is unable to provide it in the methods class because of the demands of the other content needed by the teacher candidates.

The learning objectives indicate that the teacher candidates in this class "will be proficient with technological tools, able to manage, analyze and synthesize multiple streams of simultaneous presented information and create, critique, analyze and evaluate multimedia (multimodal, new media) texts." Additionally, through this course, they will

> develop the ability to incorporate instruction in ethical use of technological tools, information literacy, and the creation, analysis, synthesis, and evaluation of multimodal texts . . . [and] develop expertise

in using digital composition tools and in producing multimodal texts, plus develop an open and receptive attitude towards learning and becoming comfortable with new technologies as they arise.

These objectives will be achieved by creating two portfolios, both in paper, comprised of "one or two 3" 3-ring (or one 4") with dividers and folders" as well as a "flashdrive," which should be brought to every class meeting. The second portfolio contains a writing section that includes a "multi-modal revision of one of your 3 major pieces from Portfolio 1," copies of all emails between the teacher candidates and an "e-mentor," a multi-media grammar lesson, and "a tech-teaching analysis [comprised of] a detailed critique of at least 5 tools (Web 2.0 sites, software, hardware, etc.)" for teaching writing.

There are several lectures on writing in a digital environment, evaluating and responding to student writing in a digital environment, multimodal composition and digital genres, and technology tools for the writing teacher. It is unclear if the class is held in a computer-enhanced space, but the presumption can be made that teacher candidates will have access to some type of computer during class time because of the requirement to have a "flashdrive" at all sessions.

Cell phone usage during class is prohibited, but this policy presumes its rudimentary use for telephoning or texting only. "[C]ell phone use or texting during class will indicate that you are not attending in good faith and will result in your being counted absent." Nonetheless, the instructor has an established student-professor communication (email policy) in that "I check and respond to email during business hours. Therefore, you should not expect a response from me on nights and weekends. I will attempt to answer all emails by the end of the following business day."

Despite the requirement to have two three-ring or one four-ring binders to keep resources and the stages of assignments, all the teacher candidates in Pre-Professional Composition and Rhetoric must also complete a Digital Portfolio. The presumption here is that once the teacher candidates have compiled their two paper portfolios, the graded or benchmarked artifacts in those two portfolios will be digitized and submitted as the Digital Portfolio. However, it is unclear when the digitized portfolio is due and if it is even due in this particular class since it does not have a due date in the course outline—only the two paper portfolios are indicated with due dates.

Standardizing Technology in English Methods

Curriculum and Methods of Teaching English is an in-person, general English methods course that integrates faith and learning. In this class, teacher candidates demonstrate "knowledge about language; literature; oral, visual, and written literacy; print and non-print media, and technology." The syllabus specifies that the course content includes teaching practices that address technology and media literacy as well as curriculum, assessment, project-based learning, and service learning. Learning objectives are indicated in a grid that clearly aligns state, national (NCTE), ISTE (International Society for Technology in Education), 21st Century Learning Skills, and Praxis II content and practice standards with the School of Education's conceptual framework called The Teacher Professional. Part of the framework indicates, "The Teacher Professional acts on a belief that all students can learn, plans instruction that addresses diversity, embeds technology, and assesses continually to ensure high levels of learning." Following this framework, specific sub-learning standards are shown in alignment with state, NCTE, ISTE, 21st Century, and Praxis II. Each assignment indicates which state, NCTE, ISTE, 21st Century, and/or Praxis II standard is met by completing that assignment. Hence, the two practice lessons, their presentations, and the five-day unit plan must meet both ISTE and 21st Century standards in addition to state, NCTE, INTASC, and Praxis II standards. Lesson plans and their presentations are guided by the university's College of Education's format and "[p]rofessional dress is required, and the use of technology is encouraged." It is presumed that technology usage here would be for presentation purposes. However, one section of the content of the plan specifies that the teacher candidates must indicate the 21st Century and Technology Tools standards addressed in the plan and address the following specific objective, "**G. Technology ([State] 1A; NCTE 3.6, 4.6; ISTE 1a, 1b, 1c):** Incorporate appropriate technology for learning, practice, projects, rewards, enrichment, review, and re-teaching." One section of the plan's rubric specifies that technology integration will be assessed as indicated in Table 4.1.

Table 4.1 Sample Rubric 3: Technology Integration (from Curriculum and Methods of Teaching English)

CATEGORY	5	4	3	2–0	Rating
Technology [State] 1A NCTE 3.6, 4.6	Tools enhance learning significantly. Strong student involvement is evident. Good choice of tools and back-up plan.	Tools enhance learning somewhat. Some student involvement and back-up plan may be evident.	Tools show little effect on learning. Student involvement and back-up plan are not evident.	Tools are not used.	

It is worth note that Curriculum and Methods of Teaching English has a concurrent 40-hour field experience, with the expectation that teacher candidates will "prepare a lesson plan and teach at least one lesson during the placement." The cooperating teacher evaluates this plan and its presentation using the College of Education's rubric for field experiences. Each section of this rubric is aligned with the state's, NCTE, InTASC, ISTE, and Praxis II standards. However, the field observation instrument does not mention technology as a stated assessment item, despite the alignment to the ISTE standards in each of the section headers. Sections include curriculum and planning, the learner and learning, teaching, and professional responsibilities but not professional dispositions. Despite the detail of the field experience rubric, grades are not determined through this rubric. There is an additional rubric that logs in all the field experience components (time sheets, daily logs, lesson evaluation, assignment sheets, and cooperating teacher evaluation) that determines the grade for performance in the placement. This rubric also has no indication of how technology integration is used to assess performance in the field and does not align its assessment items to any of the standards or school's conceptual framework. However, the omission of how technology integration fits into planning and teaching during the field experience may be indicative of a lack of access to technology in these clinicals, as mentioned earlier.

Despite the lack of explanation of how technology integration is expected or assessed in the clinical portion of this course but aligned to technology standards in the rubrics, when the teacher candidates create a 30-item resource folder due at semester's end, technology is not an assessment category although its rubric indicates alignment with ISTE standards as part of its assessment criteria. Additionally, the course calendar indicates that, early in the semester, the teacher candidates submit an annotated bibliography that lists 10 websites that address grammar instruction or knowledge. However, this assignment does not specifically appear elsewhere in the syllabus and seems additional to the 30-item resource folder.

The course calendar is organized by following the chapter outlines in Burke's *The English Teacher's Companion*. Therefore, it can be presumed there are lectures on technology when that content coincides with Burke's chapters that cover that content. Additionally, teacher candidates are sent to websites regularly to learn about standards and find models of unit planning at NCTE.

Although there is not a policy that bans the use of technology in this class per se, it seems that the course is not held in a computer-enhanced space or uses a course management system based on the descriptions of how to submit assignments. The only time technology for classroom use is mentioned is in the "Classroom Courtesy" statement. Teacher candidates are asked to avoid distracting their peers and that "[t]exting should be avoided except in rare circumstances."

Even with the heavy thread of sustained, engaged technology integration for teaching assessed throughout the rubrics for the lesson and unit plans, presentations, and field experiences, it is not clear what technology integration looks like in this class. It is never referenced for the learning experience except to go to a website to learn content.

Inconsistent Engagement With Technology to Teach English

Even though the courses detailed earlier indicated sustained, active engagement to integrate technology into the teaching practices of teacher candidates, the few technologies identified in the assignments were what Charles Bates described about his own teacher education program during his focus group interview as being "primarily" Prezi or PowerPoint presentations. Alex Terrell echoed Bates' sentiment when he mused that in his own methods courses, he felt that the teacher candidates were not "having an opportunity to really fully utilize the technology to the degree that they could." However, as discussed in Chapter 2, the open-ended questionnaire responses indicated that technology was integrated across a program, while some of the focus group discussions indicated a more robust integration of technology into teaching practices than was evident through the syllabi analysis—an observation that reinforces the limitations of solely relying on syllabi as a data source. Thus, the data sources in this study provided many levels of understanding as to what technology integration entailed, how it was defined, and how unevenly and inconsistently it can be implemented even within a singular program.

Contradictions abounded when teacher candidates were required to integrate technology into their own practices. Some portfolios were kept as paper, then digitized. Presentation software was considered integrating technology into a lesson. Some teacher candidates were prohibited from using technology during class time. Course management systems and discussion boards were not taught but assigned. These inconsistencies reflect on how English teacher educators are prepared to teach with technologies themselves, reasons that span philosophical, generational, or social reasons (see Chapter 2).

The technologies most prevalently integrated into teacher candidate teaching included rhetorically analyzing websites as new, digital texts; using presentation software or interactive whiteboards to reinforce lectures and organize information; creating and maintaining teaching portfolios; developing rubrics, and creating multimodal texts. These technologies tended to be closed spaces to assess knowledge; they rarely referenced open technologies for collaborative purposes. It was unclear if teacher candidates developed lessons that taught video or film production (except in one class), multimodal texts, online writing workshop, online tutoring, blogs and discussion boards, or other maker spaces for new knowledge or new tasks.

Despite the requirement throughout these courses for teacher candidates to integrate technology into their own lessons and unit plans, it was commonly referred to as a "tool" in assignment narratives or in the rubrics, often replicating existing pen and paper approaches to the teaching of English. Rarely did assignments reach a level of creating new content that acted interdependently to create new knowledge and new tasks (Hsieh, 2018; Mirra, 2018; Rowsell, Morrell, & Alvermann) or underscore the learning of conceptual, procedural, or attitudinal knowledge specific to the teaching of English.

Hence, in the next chapter, I will look across this study to discuss how technology integration has changed the content of the English language arts, who uses it, and to what extent it has affected the teaching of English. Chapter 5 will explore technology's (in)consistency of use and how integration continues to change our basic understanding of what is English.

References

Burke, J. (2013). *The English teachers' companion*. 4th ed. Portsmouth, NH: Heinemann.

Hsieh, B. (2018). This is how we do it: Authentic and strategic technology use by novice English teachers. *Contemporary Issues in Technology and Teacher Education*, 18(2). 271–288.

Hobbs, R. (2011). *Digital and media literacy: Connecting culture and classroom*. Thousand Oaks, CA: Corwin.

Laurillard, D. (1993). *Rethinking university teaching: A framework for the effective use of educational technology*. London, UK: Routledge.

Mirra, N. (2018, July 03). Connected learning and 21st century English teacher education [Blog post]. *Educator Innovator*. Retrieved from https://educatorinnovator. org/connected-learning-and-21st-century-english-teacher-education

Rowsell, J., Morrell, E., & Alverman, D.E. (2017). Confronting the digital divide: Debunking brave new world discourses. The *Reading Teacher*, 71(2). 157–165. doi:10.1002/trtr.1603

5 Complicating the Teaching of English

Technology and Its Integration

Tensions abound when decisions must be made as to which content needs to be taught in an English language arts methods (teaching practices) class to ensure highly qualified, effective teacher candidates certified to do "tomorrow in today's classrooms" (Morrell, 2015, p. 312). Struggling over choosing the *right* content, teacher educators are tasked with making decisions based on current theory and practice, which may then be affected by generational, philosophical, and/or social reasons. Moreover, these decisions can be constricted in part by the availability of resources and personnel, physical locations of universities, and/or the philosophical underpinnings of a program or teacher educator (Pasternak, Caughlan, Hallman, Renzi, & Rush, 2018). One area of tension is the integration of technology into the teaching and learning of English despite a consensus in the field that it is essential content that continues to change literacy practices (Pasternak et al., 2018).

Despite the challenges to support teacher candidates in teaching multi-modal literacies and technology integration, many teacher educators agree with Goodwyn (Hawthorne, Goodwyn, George, Reid, & Shoffner, 2012) and believe that the future of the English language arts classroom is "predicated on a model of English operating in a multimodal, digital environment in which students are fully engaged in a creative relationship with reading and writing all kinds of texts" (p. 299). Practical solutions to providing this content in an active, sustained manner in the methods class are complicated further due to the rapid change of technology platforms, devices, and applications. Anita Vogel, in a focus group interview, explained,

> Yeah, I mean, the English methods class is so packed it's impossible to know what to focus on. You do end up having to drop some things . . . I don't want technology to be content. I'm not teaching technology. I'm teaching students how to become teachers who are teachers of English, and primarily teachers of students, right?

Tensions such as the one described earlier affect how technology is integrated into the teaching and learning of English. When technology is taught as content, its integration should underscore the learning of conceptual, procedural, attitudinal and/or valued-based knowledge specific to the teaching of English.

In tension with Vogel's previous observation, one open-ended question respondent explained,

> My understanding is that we cannot fully address [English language arts] without acknowledging that we engage with language through various technologies, and that technological advances drive the development of language in all its uses. Integration is not optional.

For integration to happen to this level, technology should move beyond being a tool to deliver content to become content that is integral to the learning process that supports instructional practices. Technology interacts with the more traditional content of English studies (literature, composition, language, and oratory) to create new knowledge and new tasks. Integrating technology in this manner has been met to greater or lesser degrees in English teacher education programs for reasons that include the extent of access, level of understanding, instructor interest and expertise, and availability of resources and time. These conditions impact all the varied aspects of English teacher education: classroom management, content standards, the learning of students, the teaching of the content, access to platforms and applications, curriculum design, and engagement with technology's continuous change—changing English in ways many English teacher educators did not envision when they were teaching middle and secondary school. During one of the focus group interviews, Joseph Shain observed, "I think the technology throws off my students. That's the challenge that I think we have, and that integration of technology plus content is really frustrating for my teacher candidates who didn't envision that."

In this chapter, I explore the tensions found in this study in how technology has changed English as a discipline, detailing the demands placed on teacher educators to include content they are not necessarily confident in teaching, finding the time in which to provide it in a teacher education program with limited credit hours, and how this content calls for a reevaluation of English teacher identity. I then discuss how technology has been integrated into both the teaching and learning of English language arts methods classes and the effects of that integration on clinical experiences. I next examine the study's findings in alignment with the United States Department of Education's Office of Technology's National Education Technology Plans. I conclude with recommendations for English teacher education programs to support teacher educators to integrate technology. Chapter 5 explores technology's (in)consistency of use and how integration continues to change our basic understanding of what is English.

Changing English

Effectively integrating technology and valuing it as a practice has complicated how English studies are taught across K–16 levels. Teacher educators are expected to develop expertise in the more traditional content that constitutes English—literature, language, composition, oratory—but now, they must additionally develop expertise in understanding technology platforms and applications; accommodating the unequal and, sometimes, suspect funding of technology across and between school districts and universities to critically understand its usage; use standards to drive effective technology integration in education; and locate the common ground between valuing technology in the classroom and coming to terms with technology's ability to both distract or engage learners that, oftentimes, generate contradictory technology policies across educational institutions.

Time and Practice

Teacher educators acknowledge that technology integration requires time and practice to be taught effectively—time and practice often not provided through sustained professional development for teacher educators (Nelson, Voithofer, & Cheng, 2019), nor possible through an undergraduate program with an average of 4–6 credits in comprehensive content-specific methods courses (Pasternak et al., 2018). A number of respondents to the open-ended questions from the survey voiced concerns along these lines of thinking:

> [Teacher candidates] should begin to understand how these tools enhance learning, and how they change the way students learn. They should have many and multiple opportunities to experiment and play with these technologies and begin incorporating them into their written and field preparation.

Amanda Reiter, a focus group participant, echoed similar concerns,

> I often feel like I don't have enough time in my methods course to really adequately address technology. We have two methods courses, but one of them is technically our young adult literature course. I always feel like I could teach a whole course on [the English language arts] and technology integration.

In Reiter's response, as well as in the anonymous participant responses, time and practice is an important tension that limits their ability to effectively integrate technology into the English language arts. Such luxuries as having teacher candidates equipped with laptops from the first year of enrollment, universities and schools providing teacher educators professional development in technology integration, content specialists collaborating with technology specialists, universities or schools establishing a Commitment to Technology vision, and programs requiring teacher candidates to take additional technology integration classes pre-program (as was done with the integration exemplar, Teaching Writing in the Middle and Secondary Schools, see Chapter 2), are not afforded to many teacher educators, nor are such infrastructure and resources affordable by many teacher education programs.

Reevaluating English Teacher Identity

To address changes in English studies content resulting from technology integration, some teacher educators feel they must move from, or, at the very least, minimize, their focus on the more traditional content of teaching English and instead focus on the technology content. Making this kind of move is dependent upon whether teachers see value in the technology in alignment with their already established educational philosophies, a move that sometimes requires a reevaluation of their own teacher identities and philosophies of what constitutes English (Pasternak, 2007; Ottenbreit-Leftwich et al., 2015).

Reiter commented about how she feels about English changing,

> I think one of the issues I'm finding as program director is—or just an English educator—is just the competing conceptions of what it means to be an [English language arts] teacher in our current times. What I feel very strongly about is students having meaningful experiences with language and literacy and literature and different forms of communication and how that is bumping against a lot of other conceptions.

Reiter's concerns are in tension with Goodwyn's vision that English is changing to a model "operating in a multimodal, digital environment" (Hawthorne et al., 2012, p. 299). However, both see the study of English residing in a creative relationship with language and literature and the reading and writing of it.

Juggling and navigating the varied content and concerns affecting the teaching of English, teacher educators must make decisions as to what extent their programs can provide certain content in the methods class, making decisions based on their own expertise and philosophies and the location and resources offered at their universities. As to how change happens across some programs, focus group participant Sean Prinsen exclaimed, "I'm kind of astonished by the amount of integration of technology we have in our program. Largely because it almost never comes from me!" This tension has resulted in the inconsistent integration of technology to both learn English and teach English as discussed in the next section.

Which Technologies Are Used in the English Language Arts Methods Class?

English teacher educators indicate that when they address changes to disciplinary content, they do so mostly through new readings and assignments in the methods course (Pasternak et al., 2018), a practice that is contradictory to their acknowledgement that frequent exposure to and practice with technology (or any other new content, for that matter) would be more effective. This situation is particularly concerning regarding the integration of technology and the teaching of multimodal texts in the methods course. Findings show that when technology is mentioned in a syllabus, it is generally only mentioned in the course objectives or the certification standards. However, there is an understanding that technology integration should be aligned with standards, as one open-ended question respondent noted, "Using technology should always be driven by learning goals and the affordances of the technological tools to help students reach those learning goals." This understanding was seen across the syllabi analysis; but, in contrast, despite most syllabi listing technology in the course goals and objectives, it was rarely included as a topic under the assigned readings or listed in the course outline for workshopping or lecture.

If technology integration was required in the course's assignments, it was infrequently explicitly taught, described or engaged in (see Tables 2.1 and 2.4) for teaching English or learning English teaching methods. Nevertheless, based on the focus group conversations, teacher educators require their teacher candidates to integrate technology into their own teaching practices despite the syllabi analysis not upholding that finding (see Chapter 2 and Appendix regarding basing studies on syllabi as the sole source of data). However, it was apparent during the focus group conversations that teacher educators were not confident in their own abilities to teach technology integration but saw the need to structure learning environments for it to happen. Therefore, technology integration may be taught more frequently in the methods course than the syllabi demonstrate, but inconsistently so and without great confidence by the teacher educator. Prinsen explained how he teaches and supports his teacher candidates to integrate technology into their lessons,

We have students make short films and create web pages and use Skype and Schoology and other—we teach them how to use those kinds of things. I think that in our program most of the technology that happens happens in the context of fairly open-ended assignments that we give. Say, just for example, off the top of my head, you just say, 'Okay, we're gonna create a five-week Shakespeare assignment.' Okay? We have some pretty broad parameters. You have to do this, you have to do this, etcetera etcetera. Other than that, the students can do pretty much what they want. They come back with units that have technology all over the place, right? Because these are like 20-, 21-year-old young people, and they just know so much about technology. They're the ones who are so often introducing me to the technology, so I would say that yeah, we encourage the use of technology as instructors. . . . I would be lying if I said it's a huge priority for us. Okay? Rather it's our [teacher candidates] that bring it into the conversation.

Despite Prinsen creating an environment for technology exploration, it is up to the teacher candidates to decide to what extent technology affects their teaching practices. The presumption that digital natives understand technology well enough for it to become content in their lessons is not an unfamiliar attitude (see Chapter 2) and speaks to the needs of teacher candidates to look at technology integration to create new knowledge and move from it being a tool that replicates standard English language arts practices. From all stages of the study, it was clear that when technology was engaged in by teacher candidates and/or their teacher educators, it was generally for closed, assessment purposes and not open, collaborative purposes. Another focus group participant, Alex Terrell, explained,

I'd say the technology is being used in a very limited way. I'm old school; I'm back from the Super 8 movies days. Our teachers would give us a movie camera and a couple rolls of film and tell us to go out and create a visual response to a work or to a poem that we read. I don't see any kind of what I would call creative use of the technology. To me, it's more like cutting and pasting and very rudimentary type uses of the technology. I mean, it's nice to have the access to different types of information instantly, but they're not doing much with it, and they're certainly not composing with the—with some of the video programs that are available on the computer. I don't see a whole lot of creative response type use of the media and the technology.

When teacher candidates are asked to use technology for their own learning purposes—creating a portfolio or engaging in online discussion—active, extended technology integration is implicitly taught or the directions provided by the teacher educator presumes that the teacher candidates already know how to navigate the technology being used (see Chapters 2 and 3). When readings about technology were assigned, they mostly focused on multimodality and new literacies, but not integration. When web sources were linked to, they were pervasively used for finding professional resources and, when they were provided to the teacher candidates, they were frequently done so as active URL hyperlinks without webpage titles or other ownership indicators on paper syllabi.

Video recordings were used predominantly for the teacher candidates to record their own teaching moments and reflect on the effectiveness of their content and delivery, but rarely was there evidence of them being used to create videos or text. However, during the focus group interviews, Sean Prinsen described an assignment that drew together a number of technology objectives that also focused on more traditional English language arts objectives,

> We do a thing on teaching students to do rhetorical analysis by making a short film. They'll read a short story, do a rhetorical analysis of that short story. Then we have a filmmaker who works with us who teaches basic filmmaking techniques and how different film making techniques can mimic certain rhetorical strategies used by a writer. Then the students make a short film adaptation of a short story of their choice. In a sense, that's using technology to teach the content of rhetorical analysis, but on the other hand, we're teaching them basic filmmaking techniques, too. I guess that would be teaching the content, so I guess that's sort of like a hybrid.

Thus, in employing technology to create new text, the assignment replicates a standard English language arts assessment practice to do so. However, this assignment hybridizes the concept of rhetorical analysis and asks the technology and standard English language arts practice to work interdependently to learn/teach a concept.

When technology integration was mentioned in syllabi, many teacher educators posted their readings or asked for assignment submissions via course management systems, a requirement that demanded teacher candidates access technology. Paradoxically, in these same syllabi, there were statements that indicated that technology usage (computers, phones, etc.) was prohibited during class time. These policies were often mentioned alongside directions that instructed the teacher candidates to download readings, journal postings, and/or other assignments prior to class and bring them along to class as paper documents.

PowerPoint is mentioned by name as the favored presentation application, and, many times, it is the only technology requirement for the teacher candidates to integrate into lessons or to use to share their lessons for collaborative review during class—a problematic practice in classes that prohibit technology during class. However, as Amanda Reiter noted in the focus group interviews, "I really try to emphasize and have conversations with the students that it's not technology just for the sake. You can use PowerPoint and still lecture for an hour and you're not implementing technology to the way that—using technology to the ways that it can be used to enhance instruction." Another focus group participant, Joseph Shain, explained how he fits the technology requirements together during the methods class but expressed his concerns about focusing the methods class on technology integration despite acknowledging that it supports his teacher candidates' understanding of digital literacy,

> I have them use a web-based tool which is also an app called School-ogy. My students actually go in there, they find articles, digital articles to read. They link it to videos to read, they explore websites, and they have—and we respond in forums and various discussion boards. I don't really use PowerPoints. If I do use a PowerPoint, I have my students create narrated PowerPoints that they can then post to their future class web pages. To me, it's really—we do screencasts and a whole bunch of other stuff. But to me really the powerful part is I have to get my students prepared to walk into a classroom, know what blended learning is, know what a flip[ped] classroom is, know some different web-based tools that my—that they can implement right away. Because if my students go into a classroom and they don't have these just foundational digital literacy skills, they won't be successful in their internship.

Another common technology use included online discussions with practicing teachers to collaboratively mentor teacher candidates. However, online discussion was most often employed to provide a space for the teacher candidates to discuss pre-lecture readings or for the teacher educator to check if those readings occurred and/or their responses had any depth. Despite little evidence of Google Drive or Google Classroom usage in the syllabus analysis, these two Google products were mentioned repeatedly as almost a standard practice in the methods courses by the focus group participants. Website rhetorical analysis, analyzing the viability of a professional resource, seemed to be a favored assignment also.

Although online tutoring and Skype were mentioned as integrated practices by the focus group participants, there was little evidence in the syllabi of these technologies being used in the methods course. The focus group participants discussed the open, collaborative nature of such technologies, but the conversation turned to how collaborative applications can be haphazard and cause tension between the teacher education program and the field experience if the technology's use is not mutually beneficial to both the teacher education program and the K–12 school, or if the experience merely becomes a convenient tool to connect teacher candidates with high school writers who cannot travel to urban or rural locations. Sean Prinsen noticed, "as I'm sure you guys know, any time you try to do this kind of inter-institutional thing, it's just like a logistical nightmare, right?" which may be the reasoning behind these types of practices being avoided by some teacher educators.

Findings such as those described were reflected in a recent longitudinal study (Doerr-Stevens & Pasternak, in review) that investigated the experiences of English language arts teacher candidates as they engaged with web-based technology as part of their English language arts content requirements, a course that focused essentially on learning about the composing process through multimodal text creation. This ongoing study's preliminary findings indicate that once teacher candidates move into their field and student teaching placements, they mostly engage technology through closed technology for the purposes of student management (online grade books, digital submission, etc.), practices that seem to mirror those found most prevalent in the methods classes described earlier. When open technology was used, it was for ease of access to providing feedback to students through Google Drive or Classroom. Further investigation is in process, but despite having coursework that centered on creatively engaging with technology to make new knowledge and being provided the space to further develop that content in two English language arts methods classes, the teacher candidates could not find the support or the space in their field and student teaching placements to integrate it into their teaching practices. How technology is encountered and used in the clinical experience is discussed further in the next section.

Technology's Impact on Clinical Experiences

Technology integration affects not only the content of the methods courses, but the relationships that teacher education programs build with the school districts where teacher candidates are placed for fieldwork and student teaching. Shain discussed his program-community relationship and how it affected what and where he taught technology integration,

> I work in a very, very technology-rich county. My county has gone 1:1, and so every elementary school student has an iPad and every middle school student has an iPad and every high school student has a Dell

Venue. My students walk into a classroom and they're—and I'm talking about the high school now—and there's 20 students with their Dell Venues fired up and ready to go. In our program, we don't have a technology course, so what I've done in my coursework is I've kind of flipped the situation on my students [by including technology content in the human development class].

In agreement with Shain regarding program-community disparities, Terrell, observed,

[Teacher candidates are] supposed to be able to take [their technology knowledge] out into the clinical setting and, as was suggested earlier, at least meet the students in the schools where they are or allow them to take advantage of the technology that's available out in schools and not—the teacher candidate[s] not feel as if they're behind or not up to speed with the technology that's available to P12 students out in the schools.

Both Shain and Terrell acknowledge that technology integration is essential content in the school districts in which they place teacher candidates. Hence, for them, it also becomes essential content in their program classes. However, many teacher candidates use technology even less frequently in their field and student teaching placements than in their methods courses (see Table 3.1). This finding continues to create tensions between the teacher education program and the schools where teacher candidates are placed, moving teacher candidates who studied technology integration in more independent, creative ways to use it almost exclusively as closed applications for classroom management and infrastructure support (Doerr-Stevens & Pasternak, in review).

As evidenced from both Shain and Terrell's observations, there is tension concerning the inconsistent distribution of resources between the K–12 schools and university teacher education programs; some teacher educators feel dedicating time in the methods class to technology integration maybe time ill spent. Thus, under-resourced universities placing teacher candidates in appropriately resourced school districts (or the inverse) creates tensions across both institutions thinking either the teacher candidates are ill-prepared, or the community has more important educational goals. Some programs, like Amanda Reiter's (see Chapter 2), find they have to talk through technology usage and hope their teacher candidates can make use of their personal technology. Other teacher educators have pushed their universities to require teacher candidates to purchase technology as a programmatic requirement.

In a focus group conversation, Charles Bates said to Joseph Shain, "Eventually, we're going to say, 'As part of this program, you must have a'—whether it's a tablet or an iPad." Shain indicated that he was able to coerce "his college to purchase a class set of Dell Venues so I could model what's going on in the schools. I think the onus should be on the university to provide it, not the [teacher candidate]. College is expensive enough." In agreement with Shain, Anita Vogel responded,

> We're the same as well. We have tools in the classroom to model, and most of our [teacher candidates] have their own and bring it with them. But if they don't, we have a set. How are you going to model it if you don't have the tools.

Jack Akers, in another focus group discussion echoed these concerns,

> Schools are really well-equipped like no other district I've ever seen. They have everything in the classroom, including their own laptop to run the SMART board and everything, but in English, I rarely have an intern or a mentor teacher who actually used the technology. Something we do in our reading and writing classes is we talk about multimodal composition. We talk about a combination of text and image, whether it's video or anything, but we do that on campus, but then I never see it in their practice, in part because their mentor teachers aren't doing it, either.

Contrastively, other respondents felt that it was their teacher candidates who were pushing them for more technology integration. However, this push was for locating professional resources to enhance their teaching practices. Bill Warner explained,

> Our recent graduates tell us they'd really like to have more resources, more websites where they could draw teaching activities, more programs for—that they could become familiar with so that they could use them in the classroom. It's just a never-ending growth area. Our [teacher candidates] at least feel like they're not keeping up with that. It's hard. They're going to college all the time and they're using the things they have to use that are right in front of them; there's a wide variety out there that they're not aware of.

Conversely, tensions prevail when the university is technology rich, but the school district is not. In a focus group interview discussed in Chapter 2, Joseph Shain, observed that one school district he places teacher candidates in is technology rich and spends "a bajillion dollars on this technology" while another is "referred to as the corridor of shame because of the poverty levels down there, and they have—they might have pencils in the classroom." Thus, the unevenness and availability of technology across educational institutions continues to be problematic and dependent upon a community's and/or university's commitment to it or the expertise within each organization to even use it effectively. As technology integration becomes even more expected of educators in K–12 schools (USDOE OET, 2017), English teacher educators will have to determine where they have expertise and resources to support teacher candidates, what the needs are of the communities in which they place teacher candidates, and what the value is of changing the English methods course, aligning it with their own and the university's teaching philosophies. Parameters for technology integration are outlined extensively in the United States Department of Education's Office of Educational Technology National Education Technology Plans.

(In)Consistency of Technology Integration in Higher Education: The Reality of the United States Department of Education Office of Educational Technology National Education Technology Plans

The United States Department of Education's (US DOE) Office of Educational Technology (OET) is tasked to develop national educational policy and vision "for how technology can be used to transform teaching and learning and how to make everywhere, all-the-time learning possible for early learners through K–12, higher education, and adult education" (US DOE OET, What we do, n.d.). The OET attempts to achieve this through supporting equitable access to technology-based learning experiences and broadband, entrepreneurial innovation, cutting-edge research opportunities, and professional development for all teachers. In response to the United States Congress's Every Student Succeeds Act of 2015, the OET published what it considers the "flagship educational technology policy document for the United States" (USDOE NETP, 2016). In summary, the purpose of the document, and its future iterations for PK–12 and higher education (USDOE NETP, 2017; USDOE HESNTP, 2017), is to "set a national vision and plan for learning enabled by technology through building on the work of leading educational researchers; district, school, and higher education leaders, developers; entrepreneurs; and nonprofit organizations" (USDOE OET, 2016, p. 1). It is a "call to action, a vision for learning enabled through technology, [and] a collection of recommendations & [sic] real world examples" (USDOE OET, 2016, p. 2). The premise of the plan is that

> Technology can be a powerful tool for transforming learning. It can help affirm and advance relationships between educators and students,

reinvent our approaches to learning and collaboration, shrink long-standing equity and accessibility gaps, and adapt learning experiences to meet the needs of all learners.

Our schools, community colleges, adult learning centers and universities should be incubators of exploration and invention. Educators should be collaborators in learning, seeking new knowledge and constantly acquiring new skills alongside their students. Education leaders should set a vision for creating learning experiences that provide the right tools and supports for all learners to thrive.

However, to realize fully the benefits of technology in our education system and provide authentic learning experiences, educators need to use technology effectively in their practice.

(USDOE OET NTP, 2016, p. 1)

In light of this document, it is no wonder that English teacher educators are concerned that technology integration is often thought of as a panacea for education. As one open-ended question respondent acknowledged about teacher candidates, "[they] should understand why technology is important to their students' learning, should practice and interact with many different types of technology, and should plan for it in their own lessons." However, based on the focus group discussions, few participants would seem to agree with the United States Department of Education's assertion that technology "can also revolutionize the delivery of education, allow access to higher education for greater numbers of students at lower cost and with more flexibility" (USDOE HENETP, 2017, p. 9) based on their experience with it being inconsistently funded and integrated across universities and PK–12 schools. Mirra warns that the "twenty-first century learning model makes the simple assumption that the use of technology will foster innovative thinking, which, in turn, will be used to solve any intractable social problem" (2019, p. 266).

Sean Prinsen asks, "who's supplying this technology? What does this technology imply about the role of the teacher? What costs are—both literal and kind of figurative—are associated with this technology?" As evidenced from the discussion in the previous section, many universities and PK–12 schools cannot fund technology integration to effective standards. Lois Tupper, in a focus group interview, explained her concerns about creating their technology course. She mentioned that her teacher candidates,

study literacy and its relationship to technology. Ultimately, we come down on the question of are we making adaptive choices or maladaptive choices when we use technology in various ways in the classroom or in our lives? It's a more theoretical approach that asks our students to really make practical decisions in their pedagogy with foresight.

Asking teacher candidates to reflect on technology usage viability was a common integration strategy shared by the teacher educators in the focus group interviews as well as in assignments indicated in the syllabi. However, as studies support, integrating technology into the English language arts is not an intuitive process and requires time, thought, and practice. Recent studies support this need and find that if teacher educators are not professionally developed in technology integration and provided with appropriate resources, then it is unlikely their teacher candidates will value it (Nelson et al. (2019). Similarly, Ottenbreit-Leftwich, Ertmer, and Tondeur (2015) have observed that teacher candidates do not adopt technology integration themselves if their teacher educators do not emphasize its use in their methods classes. Therefore, in anticipating that teacher educators could effectively teach their teacher candidates how to "use technology to transform courses into more personal and engaging learning experiences by using digital materials to increase access and create opportunities for collaborative and project-based learning" (USDOE HENETP, 2017, p. 23) is a misinformed expectation without the teacher educators being provided the time, space, and resources to support their own learning in this area. According to the Vision statement in the United States Department of Education's "Advancing Educational Technology in Teacher Preparation: Policy Brief" (2016),

> Our students deserve to have teachers, including novice teachers, who are fully prepared to meet their needs. In today's technology rich world, that means educators need to be prepared to meaningfully incorporate technology into their practice immediately upon entering the classroom. Our nation's motivated and committed pre-service teachers deserve to be trained by faculty using technology in transformative ways that thoughtfully support and measure learning gains.
>
> (p. 4)

In this report, the United States Department of Education envisions technology integration as a panacea for future teaching. However, as Mirra (2019) notes, it is misguided to think "that integrating technology into a lesson will inherently transform traditional academic instruction into a cutting-edge, forwarding thinking learning experience" (p. 266). Moreover, with the inconsistent funding of technology across private and public universities, the cost of requiring personal technology as teacher education program admission criteria, and/or the support of faculty to learn technology skills not central to their disciplines, the NTP's vision statement seems not in reach for many teacher education programs, especially in light of the widespread defunding of public higher education continuing over the past few years across the United States. If accreditation is bestowed only upon teacher education programs that can fulfill expensive technology requirements, then there is a good chance that teachers will not be educated to serve the communities in which they are hired, nor would these universities educate a teacher workforce that demonstrates the multiple perspectives needed by our multicultural and multi-linguistic society. After all, as has been discussed, English teacher educators vary in their expertise and conceptions of the teaching of English, a field that is highly diverse and continually redefines itself as it focuses on supporting critical thinkers, speakers, writers, and readers (Pasternak et al., 2018).

Effectively Integrating Technology

Technology is ever changing our communication practices and as difficult as it is to stay current with the new hardware, software, and applications that create these new practices, it is equally challenging to integrate them into the education of future English teachers, especially in a 120-credit undergraduate course of study that must also include knowledge(s) in linguistics, language, literature, composition, theater, oratory, and/or journalism. Often, the best a teacher education program can do is support teacher candidates to become independent learners, who see the possibilities provided through experimentation and chance-taking across all the content required in their learning how to teach English. However, as Hsieh (2018) observed from studying her own teacher education program, teacher candidates need "guided opportunities to engage with technology including social media, to negotiate their own personal challenges, and to find ways in which technology (designed for classroom, professional, and personal use) can be empowering tools for their professional practice" (p. 285). Therefore, it is incumbent upon teacher education programs and their teacher educators to create spaces for deliberate, guided support for technology integration to be effectively present in practice (Hsieh, 2018; Rust & Cantwell, 2018). Regrettably, these spaces are expensive and the professional development to maintain them equally so. Furthermore, without a means to sustain technology integration support during the clinical placements, technology usage can remain more a tool that substitutes or modifies an already-established English language arts content activity (DeCoito & Richardson, 2018; Doerr-Stevens & Pasternak, in review; Hsieh, 2018) and not become the new knowledge and new tasks (Hsieh,

2018; Mirra, 2018; Rowsell, Morrell, & Alverman, 2017) called for in its most effective integration.

Effectively integrating technology and teaching it to teacher candidates becomes even more challenging in light of technology integration being a two-step process that requires teacher educators to gain proficiency in the software applications and devices on which they run. Equally challenging is what one open-ended question respondent noted in that "Teacher candidates should get hands on experience with integrating technology into their teaching and learning, so that they have had experience from both the teacher's and student's perspective of what it's like to teach and learn with technology." These skills transverse learning how to teach English, but also how to navigate an educational institution.

To further complicate what the future holds for English teachers, Lynch (2016) argues that the tomorrow of English teaching must include a compositional understanding of coding and how it mediates and shapes the everyday platforms of communication—new language skills far from the desire to teach close reading and literary analysis that brought many English teacher candidates to educational studies. Shain addressed the tension between what inspires someone to become an English teacher, "[teacher candidates] had these professors who lecture and pontificate and are the sage on the stage, and they want to go into the high school classroom and they want to teach high school English as they [were] taught college-level English literature courses." This tension—become proficient at technology integration, resort to more traditional methods of literary instruction—asks teachers to reassess their place in a classroom. Are they the person at the front of the room, or do they create maker-spaces and adopt connected learning models that undergird effective technology integration (Mirra, 2018; Rowsell et al., 2017)?

Without the infrastructure to support continuing education and provide equitable distribution of resources and expertise, technology integration and its impact on communication practices will continue to be inconsistently taught across English teacher education programs. Former United States Department of Education's Secretary John King said, "one of the most important aspects of technology in education is its ability to level the field of opportunity for students" (USDOE NETP, 2017, p. 3). However, to level the field of opportunity, education needs to be funded. At this date, even well-funded and technology-rich school districts across the United States are cutting back on technology purchases considering the extreme tax cuts that first affected public universities and are now affecting PK–12 schools (Litvinov & Flannery, 2018). Further, just purchasing technology will not ensure effective technology integration—integration that underscores the learning of conceptual, procedural, and attitudinal, and/or value-based knowledge specific to English that becomes new content that acts interdependently to create new knowledge and new tasks. Investments must be made in the people who teach this content as well.

To effectively integrate technology into a university English teacher education program, investments need to be made that might include hiring English content area faculty with expertise in technology integration or providing time for them to engage in professional development, hopefully in collaboration with technology specialists. There should be investments in future teachers by providing teacher candidates extended time in the methods courses to engage in guided practice and experimentation with technology as a creative space. However, despite these investments, these skills may not transfer to clinical placements in school districts because of uneven funding. Thus, with equitable funding in public education across levels, universities could offer continuing education programs in English teacher technology integration, providing time to create and practice assignments that are aligned with national standards and critically evaluate technology's use and usefulness. These programs could serve as professional development opportunities for teacher educators to collaborate with area teachers in this content, extending the community of learners. When technology integration is looked at as a community experience, it would be possible to support this content—but investing in people is expensive. Unfortunately, if only the purchase of technology is valued and not its critical usage, it will remain a tool that replicates or mimics standard practices that already exist. However, English teacher educators cannot do this work alone, especially as technology changes English.

References

DeCoito, I., & Richardson, T. (2018). Teachers and technology: Present practice and future directions. *Contemporary Issues in Technology and Teacher Education*, *18*(2). Retrieved from www.citejournal.org/volume-18/issue-2-18/science/teachers-and-technology-present-practice-and-future-directions

Doerr-Stevens, C., & Pasternak, D. L. (in review). Knowledge work or utilitarian tool? Leveling up the commitment to integrating technology in preservice English teacher education.

Hawthorne, S., Goodwyn, A., George, M., Reid, L., & Shoffner, M. (2012). The state of English education: Considering possibilities in troubled times. *English Education*, *44*(3), 288–311.

Hsieh, B. (2018). This is how we do it: Authentic and strategic technology use by novice English teachers. *Contemporary Issues in Technology and Teacher Education*, *18*(2), 271–288.

Litvinov, A., & Flannery, M. E. (2018, July 18). The high cost of education budget cuts. *neaToday*. Retrieved from http://neatoday.org/2018/07/16/the-high-cost-of-education-budget-cuts/

Lynch, T. L. (2016). Letters to the machine: Why computer programming belongs in the English classroom. *English Journal*, *105*(5), 95–97.

Mirra, N. (2018, July 3). Connected learning and 21st century English teacher education [Blog post]. *Educator Innovator*. Retrieved from https://educatorinnovator. org/connected-learning-and-21st-century-english-teacher-education/

Mirra, N. (2019). From connected learning to connected teaching: Reimagining digital literacy pedagogy in English teacher education. *English Education, 51*(3), April, 261–291.

Morrell, E. (2015). The 2014 NCTE presidential address: Powerful English at NCTE yesterday, today, and tomorrow: Toward the next movement. *Research in the Teaching of English, 49*(3), 307–327.

Nelson, M. J., Voithofer, R., & Cheng, S. (2019). Mediating factors that influence the technology integration practices of teacher educators. *Computers & Education, 128*, 330–344.

Ottenbreit-Leftwich, A. T., Ertmer, P. A., & Tondeur, J. (2015). Interpretation of research on technology integration in teacher education in the USA: Preparation and current practices. In P. Smeyers, D. Bridges, N. C. Burbules, & M. Griffiths (Eds.), *International handbook of interpretation in educational research* (pp. 1239–1262). New York, NY: Springer.

Pasternak, D. L. (2007). Is technology used as practice? A survey analysis of preservice English teachers' perceptions and classroom practices. *Contemporary Issues in Technology and Teacher Education* [Online serial], 7 (3), 140–157. Retrieved from www. citejournal.org/volume-7/issue-3-07/english-language-arts/is-technology-used-as-practice-a-survey-analysis-of-pre-service-english-teachersperceptions-and-classroom-practices

Pasternak, D. L., Caughlan, S., Hallman, H., Renzi, L., & Rush, L. (2018). *Secondary English teacher education in the United States*. Reinventing Teacher Education Series. London, UK: Bloomsbury Academic.

Rowsell, J., Morrell, E., & Alverman, D. E. (2017). Confronting the digital divide: Debunking brave new world discourses. *The Reading Teacher, 71*(2), 157–165. doi:10.1002/trtr.1603

Rust, J., & Cantwell, D. (2018). No one fits in a box: Preservice teachers' evolving perceptions of self and others. *Contemporary Issues in Technology and Teacher Education*, 18 (2). 313–342. Retrieved from www.citejournal.org/volume-18/issue-2-18/english-language-arts/no-one-fits-in-a-box-preservice-teachersevolving-perceptions-of-self-and-others

United State Department of Education. (2016). *US Department of Education's "Advancing Educational Technology in Teacher Preparation: Policy Brief"*. Retrieved from https://tech.ed.gov/teacherprep/

United States Department of Education, Office of Educational Technology. (2016). Future ready learning: Reimagining the role of technology in education. *2016 National Technology Plan*. US Department of Education. Retrieved from http:// tech.ed.gov

United States Department of Education, Office of Educational Technology. (2017). *National Education Technology Plan*. Retrieved from https://tech.ed.gov

United States Department of Education, Office of Educational Technology. (2017). Reimaging the role of technology in higher education. *A Supplement to the National Education Technology Plan*. Retrieved from https://tech.ed.gov

Appendix
A Brief Discussion of Research Design

This appendix briefly addresses the methodology employed in a nation-wide study of English teacher education concerning the technology data collected from it. For a more detailed description of the entire study and its limitations, please see Pasternak, Caughlan, Hallman, Renzi, and Rush (2018) and Caughlan et al. (2017).

Creating the Contact List

To create a distribution list for this study, a catalog of English teacher educators from across the United States was developed with the help of colleagues who volunteered for this work and student research assistants. The catalog was compiled by reviewing each state's list of approved English teacher education certification programs recorded on the United States Department of Education's Title II (2018) website and then visiting each program's own website in search of contact information for a program representative—either an email address or telephone number. When only a phone number was available, one of the researchers telephoned for a specific email address for the program's representative. Contact information was amassed for 747 programs from the 1085 private and public institutions certifying English teachers at that time. Some programs, particularly alternative programs not affiliated with universities and colleges, had no contact information and could not be included in the contact list.

Study Design, Distribution, and Collection of Data

There were four parts to the study: 1) a contact list of English teacher educators from across the United States, 2) a questionnaire with multiple choice and open-ended questions, 3) syllabi of methods courses, and 4) focus group interviews. All parts of the study met with Internal Review Board approval at the University of Wisconsin-Milwaukee, Michigan State University,

Table A1 Study Timeline

Year 1	Create a contact list of English teacher educators across the United States
	Literature review of studies of the English language arts methods courses
	Questionnaire design and pre-testing
Year 2	Questionnaire administration and collection of syllabi
	Questionnaire analysis
Year 3	Focus group question design and pre-testing
	Focus group administration
	Syllabi and focus group analysis
Year 4	Questionnaire, syllabi, and focus group response alignment regarding technology data
	Analysis of technology data

University of Kansas, Westchester State University of Pennsylvania, and the University of Wyoming.

The questionnaire was comprised of four sections (Caughlan et al., 2017; Pasternak et al., 2018) that addressed programmatic conditions: 1) structure and design including clinical experiences; 2) teaching of four focal areas: disciplinary literacy, content-area standards, linguistic diversity, and technology integration; 3) response to conceptual, curricular, political, and institutional pressures on the field; and 4) demographic information about the respondents and their teaching situations.

The questionnaire was comprised of 90 fixed, multiple choice, and partially structured, open-ended questions, some of which were randomly distributed to the participants. It was distributed via email by the National Council of Teachers of English's Conference on English Education (CEE) (now named English Language Arts Teacher Educators [ELATE]); respondents self-administered the questionnaire over the internet.

The questionnaire included contingency questions, which allowed respondents to skip questions that were not relevant to the design of their programs. Such as, if a program only certified English teachers at the undergraduate level, the respondent could skip the questions about master's level certification, etc. Additionally, the open-ended focal area questions were randomly distributed to ease participant response time since the questionnaire could take 20–45 minutes to complete. These contingencies were put into place to reduce response burden (Barrett, 2008; Blair, Czaja, & Blair, 2014; Manski & Molinari, 2008; Sheehan, 2001). Additionally, at the conclusion of the questionnaire, also to avoid the limitations of straight survey research (Blair et al., 2014; Groves, Cialdini, & Couper, 1992; Weisberg, 2005), respondents had the option to voluntarily upload copies of their methods course syllabi. These were then de-identified by graduate research assistants.

The questionnaire was piloted with 17 volunteer English teacher educators from across the country who directed programs that varied in design and scope, and the instructors had mixed expertise across the focal areas. The piloters provided feedback on the questionnaire, which allowed for revision and clarification of the study.

Two-hundred forty-two responses, a rate of 32.4%, were collected. There was an average of 200 responses across the different focal areas. However, the responses to the technology portion of the questionnaire dropped to only 175. This lower response rate might have to do with the technology section coming toward the end of the questionnaire or due to respondent confusion with the questionnaire's use of the terms *open* and *closed* technology, although this confusion was not evident during the piloting of the study.

The lower response rate may also be indicative of the respondents having less knowledge about technology teaching and learning then they did with the other focal areas of the questionnaire, which could be caused by the technology classes often being taught separately from the methods course or respondents not having expertise in the two-step process of technology integration described in Chapter 2 and Chapter 5. Of the 175 responses to the technology portion of the questionnaire, there were 84 responses to the open-ended questions about technology integration. Of the 136 syllabi collected for the study, only two showed no evidence of technology integration being addressed (see Table 2.4).

Analysis of Data

The questionnaire underwent descriptive analysis of the quantitative data (Johnson & Christensen, 2014), with frequency data tabulated for all questions, and variables added for "check all that apply" categories to gauge the number of options chosen (see Pasternak et al., 2018 for detailed analysis across all types of questions). I coded the technology integration open-ended-question responses inductively (Bogdan & Biklen, 2011). These were not double-coded and were used primarily to illuminate quantitative results and expand the analysis of the syllabi and focus group data.

After the syllabi were de-identified by a graduate assistant, another graduate assistant and I read each one using the four-point scale described in Table 2.3 to determine its placement on the scale. Our interrater reliability was checked. Disagreements were resolved by us recoding the syllabus under discrepancy. Frequency counts were tabulated and percentages were used to support findings regarding technology integration. I used the level 4 syllabi to create the cases used throughout Chapters 2, 3, and 4. I also used the syllabi as a source of assignments, assessments, and assigned readings throughout the book. These were tabulated through Dedoose data analysis software.

The analysis of the questionnaire led to the focus group interviews (Vaughn, Schumm, & Sinagub, 1996). As mentioned earlier, these data were collected to avoid the limitations of straight survey research, including discrepant interpretations of questions and respondent fatigue (Blair et al., 2014; Groves et al., 1992; Weisberg, 2005), and the distortions of studies relying on publicly-available materials and syllabi (e.g., NCTQ, 2018) (discussed here and in Chapters 2 and 5).

The focus groups were conducted by graduate assistants over the internet using video conferencing technology. The audio portion of the interviews were recorded. Focus group participants volunteered for interviews by providing their contact information at the conclusion of the survey. The 22 participants were selected to reflect a range of program locations and design. Participants were randomly assigned to six different 45-minute interviews and posed different sets of six semi-structured interview questions. Two of the six focus groups focused specifically on technology integration, being asked:

1. The teaching of multiple literacies, multimodal texts and digital learning is changing the teaching of the English language arts. Forty percent of our respondents indicated that they integrate technology knowledge throughout their programs. How is this response consistent with your program?
2. Much of the technology used in the teaching of English language arts asks teacher candidates to work collaboratively or independently. Additionally, technology is used to teach content but also to be content. What are you teaching throughout your program that addresses technology learning in these various ways?

After introducing themselves and describing their programs, participants discussed their philosophies regarding technology integration and literacy, the way in which programs address change in information technology, and the types of technology used in programs. The other two questions dealt with another focal area. The final interview question, "What other conceptual or practical challenges do you face as a program director or a methods course instructor that you want to raise at this point?" allowed for the participants to bring up focal areas not specifically brought up in the other interview questions. Thus, in the other four interviews, technology integration came up in discussion also through this final question.

After the interviews, the recordings were transcribed and coded deductively to better link the questionnaire and syllabus analysis and inductively coded to discover issues that were not explicitly addressed by the previous analyses. These interviews allowed for another layer of understanding regarding the tensions involved in technology integration into the English language arts. Synthesizing the data from the different phases of the study allowed for a clearer picture of challenges and rewards to understanding how technology is changing the field of English teaching.

Limitations of Syllabus Analysis

Although this study was modeled after Smagorinsky and Whiting's (1995), it became clear that findings could not be derived from just one data source: syllabi. Syllabi tend to be idiosyncratic documents, sometimes controlled by university mandate, an instructor's philosophical underpinnings or inexperience in creating one, or ability to post clarifying materials digitally. When Smagorinsky and Whiting (1995) conducted their study, the syllabus was the major repository for course content. This is no longer the case. Thus, limiting this study to syllabi would have provided a limited portrait of how technology is integrated into English teacher education today.

Relying solely on syllabi as sources of data raised questions about the reliability and validity of other studies of teacher education, in particular, the National Council on Teacher Quality, "an organization that has relied solely on collecting syllabi and treating teacher educators as hostile witnesses in their reports ranking teacher education programs" (Pasternak et al., 2018, p. 160).

In determining that syllabi are inconsistent sources of data, I backward-traced syllabi to questionnaire responses and forward-traced syllabi to focus group responses, finding some inconsistencies between the questionnaire, syllabi, and focus group interviews that complicated the findings, especially in relation to technology integration. It was through all the phases of data collection for this study on technology integration that it was possible to provide this portrait detailing the rewards and challenges in changing English.

References

Barrett, K. (2008). Contingency question. In P. J. Lavrakas (Ed.), *Encyclopedia of Survey Research Methods* (p. 143). Thousand Oaks, CA: Sage.

Blair, J., Czaja, R., & Blair, E. (2014). *Designing surveys: A guide to decisions and procedures*. Los Angeles, CA: Sage.

Bogdan, R. C., & Biklen, S. K. (2011). *Qualitative research for education: An introduction to theories and methods*. New York, NY: Prentice Hall.

Caughlan, S., Pasternak, D. L., Hallman, H. L., Renzi, L., Rush, L., & Frisby, M. (2017). How English language arts teachers are prepared for twenty-first century classrooms: Results of a National Study. *English Education, 49*(3), April, 265–297.

Groves, R. M., Cialdini, R. B., & Couper, M. P. (1992). Understanding the decision to participate in a survey. *The Public Opinion Quarterly, 56*(4), 475–495.

Johnson, R. B., & Christensen, L. (2014). *Educational research: Quantitative qualitative, and mixed approaches*. Thousand Oaks, CA: Sage.

Manski, C. E., & Molinari, E. (2008). Skip sequencing: A decision in questionnaire design. *Annals of Applied Statistics, 2*(1), 264–285.

National Council on Teacher Quality (NCTQ). (2018). Raising the bar on teacher prep. *Teacher Prep Review*. Retrieved from www.nctq.org/review/home

Pasternak, D. L., Caughlan, S., Hallman, H., Renzi, L., & Rush, L. (2018). *Secondary English teacher education in the United States*. Reinventing Teacher Education Series. London, UK: Bloomsbury Academic.

Sheehan, K. (2001). E-mail survey response rates: A review. *Journal of Computer-Mediated Communication, 6*(2). Retrieved from https://onlinelibrary.wiley.com/doi/full/10.1111/j.1083-6101.2001.tb00117.x

Smagorinsky, P., & Whiting, M. (1995). *How English teachers get taught: Methods of teaching the methods class*. Urbana, IL: Conference on English Education and National Council of Teachers of English.

United States Department of Education, Office of Postsecondary Education. (2018). Enrollment in teacher preparation programs. *Title II Higher Education Act*. Retrieved from https://title2.ed.gov/Public/Home.aspx

Vaughn, S., Schumm, J., & Sinagub, J. (1996). *Focus Group Interviews in Education and Pyschology*, New York, NY: Sage.

Weisberg, H. E. (2005). *The total survey error approach: A guide to the new science of survey research*. Chicago, IL: UCP.

Index

Printed in the United States
by Baker & Taylor Publisher Services